REVOLT AGAINST REGULATION

REVOLT
AGAINST
REGULATION

The Rise and Pause of the Consumer Movement

MICHAEL PERTSCHUK

University of California Press
Berkeley • Los Angeles • London

University of California Press
Berkeley and Los Angeles, California

University of California Press, Ltd.
London, England

Library of Congress Cataloging in Publication Data

Pertschuk, Michael, 1933–
  Revolt against regulation.

  Includes index.
  1. Consumer protection—United States. 2. Trade
regulation—United States. 3. Business and politics—
United States. 4. United States—Politics and government
—1945–   . I. Title.
HC110.C63P45   381'.32'0973   82-40108
ISBN 0-520-04824-5   AACR2

Printed in the United States of America

1 2 3 4 5 6 7 8 9

To Anna

"One of man's greatest obligations is anger."

Nikos Kazantzakis,
The Last Temptation of Christ

CONTENTS

PREFACE

This book might well have been dedicated jointly to Jimmy Carter and Ronald Reagan; to President Carter for allowing me to serve as FTC chairman; to President Reagan for allowing me to stop. What had begun in 1977 as the fulfillment of an adult fantasy to lead the FTC as a legion in the consumer crusade had, four years later, lapsed into a succession of inglorious retreats.

No sooner had Reagan taken office than the commission was seized by the condition Lincoln diagnosed in his generals as "the slows." This was, of course, bad news for the nation's consumers. But for me the Reagan ascendency and my new status as just plain commissioner, unencumbered by the burdens of managing the agency, provided a "window of opportunity" for involuntary leisure and reflection.

I had been at work nearly twenty years at what I chose to believe was the public interest, mostly in promoting and shaping consumer laws for Senator Warren Magnuson and the Senate Commerce Committee he chaired. Through the sixties and well into the seventies, the consumer enterprise had flourished as we produced one new consumer law after another, defying the conventional view of a Congress far more responsive to business demands than consumer needs. Then, in the late seventies, the consumer cause had suffered a series of setbacks and defeats and, finally, the Reagan election.

It was time to look back. What had we accomplished? Where had we gone wrong? What had we learned? What next?

1

Of course, one can hardly spend twenty years in any venture without cultivating cherished notions, random insights, prejudices, debts, scores to settle—and war stories.

To force myself to organize these thoughts with some measure of discipline and coherence, I accepted the generous invitation of the Graduate School of Business Administration at Berkeley to deliver a series of lectures in the fall of 1981. This book is largely based on those lectures, expanded and edited to take advantage of the reactions and critiques of friends and colleagues to the "discussion drafts."

I am indebted widely and deeply for help: first, to Thomas Jorde, Robert Harris, and Robert Reich, who nurtured the embryonic lectures and to Dean Earl Cheit and Richard Haber at the Business School, my gracious hosts in Berkeley.

To my former comrades in arms at the FTC, especially Michael Sohn and Bill Baer, whose memories proved more reliable, if not rosier, than mine. To my staff as minority commissioner, shrunken in numbers, but expansive in energy and spirit, who hammered the early drafts into some coherence and shape: Eddie Correia, Darlene Frye, Michael Rodemeyer, William Rothbard, Judy Appelbaum, Cynthia Ingersoll, Millie Taylor, Dianne Gale, and Judy Hare.

For their reactions, corrections, inspired insights, cautionary exclamations, for pointing me past analytical barriers and historic footfalls: Charles Lindblom, Nelson Polsby, Robert Engler, Aaron Wildavsky, Thomas Whiteside, Jeremy Brecher, Steve Kelman, David Burnham, Michael Horowitz, Jacques Feuillan, Kenneth Davidson, William Kovacic, Linda Garcia.

Throughout the writing of the book, I suffered a near fatal tendency to elephantine verbiage, adjectival excess, the endless sentence and the clarity-defying metaphor. With firm but delicate pruning shears, Peter Dreyer and Jill Cutler cleared the forest.

Throughout, Stan Chesler served our joint effort as my research assistant, bringing order to chaos, bearing tedious tasks with endless good cheer, offering encouragement, stoking the fires of conviction.

I also want especially to thank James Clark, director, and Marilyn Schwartz and Amanda Mecke of the University of California Press for their commitment to the book and their energy and determination to make it work.

My wife Anna Sofaer, to whom this book is dedicated, my son and daughter Mark and Amy and my stepson Daniel, cheered me on, raised my spirits, punctured my inflation.

Throughout I have shamelessly appropriated, consciously and unconsciously, the contributions of many nameless colleagues on the Senate Commerce Committee and the Federal Trade Commission, in the press, among the bar and, yes, even among the lobbyists. From them I ask forgiveness for unintended slights and lamely extend my blanket gratitude.

It was Daniel who, sharing the blows of a mean-spirited Congress, asked one morning at breakfast, "If the FTC is an arm of Congress, how come Congress wants to break its arm for making a fist?"

That question serves as well as any as preface to this book.

On the Side of the Angels:
Congress and the Consumer in the 1960s

INTRODUCTION

One day in the winter of 1979–1980—the winter of Congress's discontent with the Federal Trade Commission—an old friend, a scholar, cornered me on a downtown street in Washington and plied me with spirited consolation. "Remember the words of the great statesman," he said. "Many enemies, much honor!" I liked that. We certainly qualified for the former; we could at least lay claim to the latter.

"I must use that line in my speeches," I gushed. "Who said it?"

He grinned, and with feigned innocence replied, "Mussolini!"

Today, in the high noon of business's triumphant regulatory revolt, a (mostly) unrepentant regulator sometimes feels as out of joint as a cashiered general dwelling on past glories. In fact, the FTC's punishing battles with Congress in the late seventies are the subject matter of much of this book. But so, too, are the early victories of the consumer movement—or, perhaps more precisely, the consumer impulse—that waxed in the ascendancy during the 1960s.

Congress enacted more than twenty-five consumer, environmental, and other social regulatory laws between 1967 and 1973. We now have a Congress hostile to all forms of government interference with business autonomy, however, making the political environment that then proved so hospitable to regulation appear strange and remote. To recapture that era of consumer influence, we might

5

begin with a brief legislative chronicle typical of the consumer protection, environmental, occupational health and safety, and other social regulatory legislation enacted by Congress during the mid-1960s through the early 1970s—the chronicle of the Flammable Fabrics Act amendments of 1967, not the most significant of these laws, but typical in genesis.

Early in 1967, a young Seattle pediatrician, Dr. Abraham Bergman, came to Washington to see Warren Magnuson, then senior senator from the state of Washington and chairman of the Senate Commerce Committee. He came to tell of the chronic, unrelenting procession of burned and scarred children through the burn center of Seattle's Children's Hospital. Why couldn't the Federal Trade Commission, which then administered the Flammable Fabrics Act,[1] mandate flame-resistant children's clothing, especially sleepwear? And if the Federal Trade Commission lacked the authority or the will, perhaps Senator Magnuson could offer legislation to see that children were adequately protected.

To us, the staff of the newly christened consumer subcommittee of the Commerce Committee, Senator Magnuson assigned the task of responding to the doctor's concerns. A quick reading of the Flammable Fabrics Act of 1953 revealed that it was hopelessly inadequate to control those cotton flannels and other textiles whose explosive flammability had led to the stream of victims in the Seattle burn center. On February 16, 1967, Senator Magnuson introduced the Flammable Fabrics Act amendments of 1967 to provide the Federal Trade Commission (later the Consumer Product Safety Commission) with broad authority to set flammability standards adequate to eliminate "the unreasonable risk" of burn injuries.

The professional staff members of the House Commerce Committee, our House counterparts, scoffed. Their committee was dominated by conservatives from Southern and border cotton and textile vending states (a political block now accorded great deference by political analysts as the "bollweevils"). And the lobbyists for the cotton textile industry warned us ominously that "blood would run in the halls of Congress" before any such legislation passed.

They were wrong. After a modest two-day hearing, the Senate Commerce Committee unanimously reported the bill to the floor, where it was passed on July 27th by voice vote. While consideration by the House Commerce Committee produced mild grumbling and

---

1. Flammable Fabrics Act, ch. 164, 67 Stat. 111 (1953).

some delay, the bill was reported to the House, passed the House, emerged from a Senate-House conference committee substantially as introduced by Senator Magnuson, and was signed into law by President Lyndon Johnson on December 14, 1967.

At the bill-signing ceremony, President Johnson, with his good friend Senator Magnuson at his side, proclaimed, "The American people are sick of seeing their children needlessly burned. This legislation is a major achievement for consumers. It provides them with the protection they need and want. I thank the Congress for passing this part of my consumer agenda."[2] For Senator Magnuson and his staff, the only mildly discordant note was the president's habitual insistence on claiming credit for the genesis of the legislation. In almost all other respects, we could take great satisfaction in our handiwork. We never doubted that what we had done would save lives and spare misery. We had challenged and defeated the forces of darkness—that is, the cotton textile industry, which had demonstrated insensitivity at best to the hazards of its products.

As congressional staff members, we had met the then prevalent measure of legislative productivity: to the procession of consumer laws that bore witness to the initiative of Warren Magnuson and the Senate Commerce Committee, we had added yet another. We enjoyed a sense of power, and we never doubted that we had employed that power in the public interest. Senator Magnuson was enshrined, first by Drew Pearson, later by Jack Anderson, as a hero of the people. The *Washington Post* and other media hailed the enactment of the Flammable Fabrics Act as a virtuous and humanitarian achievement. Ultimately, though not with good grace, the textile industry accepted the inevitability of regulation: their mood was "sullen but not mutinous."

There was a great headiness about our work in those days, for we believed that we had successfully defied the widely cited principle that in any confrontation between the interests of producers and those of consumers, the former are bound to prevail. And we—a handful of senators and their staffs—had done so without lobbies, grassroots organization, campaign contributions, or access to the great lawyer-lobbying resources of Washington.

In recent years I have come greatly to respect the insights of the

2. U.S., President, *Public Papers of the President of the United States* (Washington, D.C.: Office of the *Federal Register*, National Archives and Record Service, 1953–), p. 1138.

political scientist and economist Charles E. Lindblom, whose *Politics and Markets* seems uniquely to capture and order my experience.[3] But in 1967 I would have dismissed as archaic his grim portrait of business's political privilege and disproportionate influence on government decision making, and of the inexorable deflection of the regulatory impulse, however spontaneous, by the needs and demands of business.

The performance of the Eighty-third Congress (and the Senate Commerce Committee), in which the *first* Flammable Fabrics Act was enacted in 1953, fits squarely within Lindblom's analytical framework. That Congress had been forced to respond to the spontaneous national outrage at highly publicized, traumatic instances of child burnings caused by explosively flammable cowboy shirts and sweaters, mostly imported, dramatized by the press as "torch sweaters." Congress had responded, in its own fashion, with minimal legislation, drafted by the cotton textile industry working together with compliant Senate and House members. The legislation codified the specific, extremely modest, industry-developed voluntary standard for flammability—a standard that would prohibit only the most explosively flammable fabrics (chiefly imports). Although the Federal Trade Commission was charged with enforcing the act, the new law did not delegate any authority to strengthen the standard should it prove inadequate.

Through the 1950s and early 1960s, the Commerce Committee was hardly noted for its enterprise in pursuing consumer interests. Indeed, its primary occupation was the protection of business interests (aviation, trucking, water carriage) in the manner described by Lindblom. The members of the committee were grouped by political cognoscenti as "trucker [or teamster] senators," "railroad senators," "marine senators," and so on. As Earle Clements, former senator and chief lobbyist for the Merchant Marine Institute once told me, "Membership on the Commerce Committee assures the comfortable participation by many in one's campaigns for reelection."

Even ostensible consumer protection bills were inspired and shaped by industry. Often they reflected the efforts of one industry or one segment of an industry to eliminate "unfair competition" by another, as in the Wool Products Labeling Act,[4] designed to enhance the merchantability of virgin wool over the recycled fiber.

---

3. Lindblom, *Politics and Markets* (New York: Basic Books, 1977).
4. Wool Products Labeling Act of 1939, ch. 871, 54 Stat. 1128.

Similarly, the Fur Products Labeling Act[5] was designed to defend the fur industry against simulated fur garments, leading to the quixotic FTC challenge to the use of the term *Red Fox* in the brand name of a venerable Georgia overall manufacturer.

As late as 1963, the dominant consumer issue before the committee was pending legislation to preserve retail price fixing through federal preemption of state laws barring the enforced maintenance of retail prices. To render that disreputable remnant of recession-inspired price fixing less obviously onerous, the committee seriously entertained a series of euphemisms for price-fixing legislation: "fair trade," "quality stabilization," and, finally, in desperation, "truth in pricing." My predecessor as consumer counsel for the committee (though that was only a minor sub-assignment) assured me that I had landed a choice staff assignment, since the staff member responsible for managing the retail price maintenance legislation was assured a bountiful supply of sample price-fixed products, from toasters to audio equipment, a welcome and entirely acceptable staff "perk" in the prevailing ethical climate of the time.

Those businessmen and others who dread the growth and exuberant energy of congressional staffs doubtless will find comforting the fact that the Commerce Committee's total professional staff in 1961 numbered six, and they shared a single secretary—some rough measure of their productivity. Since bills and reports were all written "downtown" by the counsel for whichever trade association emerged from industry conflict triumphant, there was little need for independent staff resources.

By 1966, however, we were confident that such industry dominance of congressional decision making was only a rude and unlamented memory. Severe Marxist historians such as Gabriel Kolko have sought to debunk such celebrated curbs on corporate power as the Interstate Commerce Act (1887) and the Federal Trade Commission Act (1914) as business-shaped, if not business-inspired.[6] But how do they account for the strong and genuine consumer impulse of the late 1960s?

One answer has come from James Q. Wilson in *The Politics of Regulation*.[7] Wilson attributes the surge of consumer, environmen-

5. Fur Products Labeling Act, ch. 298, 65 Stat. 175 (1951).
6. Kolko, *The Triumph of Conservatism: A Reinterpretation of American History, 1900–1916* (New York: Macmillan Co., 1963).
7. Wilson, ed., *The Politics of Regulation* (New York: Basic Books, 1980).

tal, civil rights, and health and safety regulatory initiatives of the
1960s and early 1970s to the rise of what he has aptly labeled "entrepreneurial politics." We would have recognized ourselves in his
description:

> A policy may be proposed that will confer general (though perhaps
> small) benefits at a cost to be borne chiefly by a small segment of
> society. When this is attempted, we are witnessing *entrepreneurial
> politics*. . . . Since the incentive to organize is strong for opponents of
> the policy but weak for the beneficiaries, and since the political sys-
> tem provides many points at which opposition can be registered, it
> may seem astonishing that regulatory legislation of this sort is ever
> passed. It is, and with growing frequency in recent years—but it
> requires the efforts of a skilled entrepreneur who can mobilize latent
> public sentiment (by revealing a scandal or capitalizing on a crisis),
> put the opponents of the plan publicly on the defensive (by accusing
> them of deforming babies or killing motorists), and associate the leg-
> islation with widely shared values (clean air, pure water, health and
> safety). The entrepreneur serves as the vicarious representative of
> groups not directly part of the legislative process.[8]

Peter Schuck, writing in the *Yale Law Journal*, builds upon
Wilson's concept of entrepreneurial politics by observing that the
public-interest entrepreneurs succeeded because they evoked a responsive chord in the emerging "dominant vision of the larger
society":

> Finally, and perhaps most importantly, American society appears to
> have come to a new view of the role and possibilities of law and
> politics in the pursuit of the good society. . . . Today, injustices are
> readily perceived, their tractability is widely assumed, and collective
> intervention by legal rule appears to be the remedy of choice. As our
> perception of imperfection has grown, our tolerance for it has dimin-

8. Ibid., p. 370. The concept of successful consumer advocacy as an example of
"entrepreneurial politics" serves another useful analytical purpose. It has become
customary to refer to the "consumer movement." However, if we understand a
movement to reflect not only widespread popular support but, like the "populist
movement" of the late nineteenth century, an organized grassroots effort that, for its
members, transcends all other political identity or involvement, it cannot be said that
a consumer movement has ever existed. For consumer issues by their nature—unlike
wages and job security in the labor movement, for example—rarely assume priority
among citizens' competing economic concerns. Consumer issues may dominate the
political agenda under special circumstances, as in rent strikes and campaigns for rent
control laws, or, in locally organized campaigns to combat red lining in mortgage
loans or auto insurance. For certain groups, in particular the elderly on fixed incomes,
whose principal economic concern is stretching static limited income, consumer

ished. These attitudes no doubt reflect a complex evolution in morality, ideas, and politics. Whatever their cultural sources, they have fused in a melioristic, not to say utopian, ambition to reform a disagreeable social reality through the affirmative application of public power.[9]

Ironically, Wilson and Schuck, publishing in 1980 and 1981, may have captured the essence of a phenomenon that had already vanished. For if Lindblom and Kolko allow no space for the ascendance of entrepreneurial politics, by 1980 the public-interest entrepreneurs appear to have lapsed into a state of political insolvency. And a very different public vision is commonly believed to have emerged (or reemerged): rancorously individualistic, disaffected with government, especially the federal government, and nowhere more disenchanted than with regulation—what the late *Washington Star* would have characterized as a "public howl" against regulation. Lindblom's portrayal of business influence now seems precisely drawn to the scale of a Reagan administration and a Congress harmoniously attuned to business volitions:

> In American law the corporation is a 'person' . . . but these fictitious persons are taller and richer than the rest of us and have rights that we do not have. Their political impact differs from and dwarfs that of the ordinary citizen.[10]

Lindblom observes that businessmen enjoy a privileged position of influence upon public decision making, even if they never lift a finger in direct political action, because government officials know that jobs and prosperity in our economic system depend upon the successful performance of business.[11] Businessmen's demands on government are thus understandably treated with great deference

---

issues may indeed loom large. But by and large the individual consumer stake in the pursuit of consumer laws and regulations lacks the motivating energy of true political movements. The reasons that this is almost inevitably so do not reflect public ambivalence about consumer initiatives, but the limited economic stake each consumer has in each of the discrete issues that, taken together, have been viewed as consumer legislation.

9. Schuck, review of Wilson, ed., *The Politics of Regulation*, *Yale Law Journal* 90 (1981): 725.

10. Lindblom, *Politics and Markets*, p. 5.

11. Lindblom states: "Ordinarily [corporate interests] need only point to the cost of doing business, the state of the economy's stability and growth on their profits or sales prospects—and simply predict, not threaten, that adverse consequences will follow on a refusal of their demands" (ibid., p. 185).

by politicians, who well understand the causal link between continued prosperity and reelection. And in times of economic stress and insecurity, few politicians have the temerity to challenge any discrepancy that may exist between business's demands and business's legitimate needs. So we would expect Congress to be readily responsive to the complaints of business that the FTC or regulatory initiatives threaten jobs, growth, or productivity, even if the complaining businesses raise no direct threat of political retribution.

But business *has* lifted a finger. To the privileged position business enjoys by virtue of its economic role in our society one now has to add recent aggressive business political mobilization, from political action committees (PACs) to organized grassroots lobbying. It follows that fewer and fewer members of Congress are inclined to challenge business demands for relief from regulation, no matter how flimsy or disingenuous such claims may be.

The tumultuous changes in both the experience and theory of business's impact on government that have taken place in less than two decades plainly caution humility in generalizing about the politics of regulation. This is especially true for me, as one who as late as 1977 confidently operated on the premise that a potent consumerism had come to form part of the bedrock of regulatory politics, only to find it shifting radically beneath his feet.

Lindblom is essentially right: *over time*, significant government decision making affecting the interests of producers and consumers will normally respond to the needs and demands of business. But Wilson and Schuck are also partly correct in arguing that consumer-responsive politics can prevail when the political winds are right. Even at the zenith of Congress's consumer impulse, however, entrepreneurial politics posed a far more modest challenge to business autonomy and profitability than the latter writers suggest.

It is true that, in the 1960s and early 1970s, Warren Magnuson, Ralph Nader, and a handful of other consumer advocates both within and outside Congress succeeded in advancing legislative and regulatory initiatives against the determined opposition of business. But these successes were possible only through a rare, if not unique, concurrence of economic and political conditions, and they were limited by the relatively crude means available to the entrepreneurs—chiefly the evocation and exploitation of broad, consensual public outrage through empathetic media. They were also limited by ideological constrictions on the legitimacy of government intervention in the marketplace.

THE 1960S AS A FERTILE SEEDBED FOR THE NOURISHMENT
OF CONSUMER ENTREPRENEURIAL POLITICS

For consumer entrepreneurial politics to succeed in the 1960s, consumer goals had to harmonize with public attitudes and the political environment. They did. The postwar quarter century was a period of sustained, apparently boundless and real, economic growth. Largely as a consequence, the prevailing public mood in the mid-1960s remained buoyant, confident, generous.

The public agenda was the liberal agenda, the unfinished work of true grassroots movements—the labor movement, the civil rights movement—secured on the national agenda by F. D. R. and John F. Kennedy. L. B. J.'s Great Society confidently undertook the elimination of poverty. Government, preeminently the federal government, was the acknowledged and accepted instrument of social justice.

At the same time, prevailing public attitudes toward business were curiously schizoid. There was a fundamental, if unarticulated, faith in the capacity of business to perform its function in our society. As social psychologist Daniel Yankelovich observes:

> Virtually all of us presupposed that our economy would continue to function automatically and successfully, as surely as the sun would rise each morning without effort on our part. . . . Americans had grown used to the idea that the giant corporations, the government and other economic institutions would simply and eternally be there—to support the aged, build the infrastructure, create jobs, turn out wealth and do the country's work, as much a part of nature as trees and rainfall from heaven. [12]

This uncritical faith was ironically nowhere more manifest than among the advocates of consumer protection and environmental legislation. For though we might question the good faith of corporate commitment to the consumer and the environment, we never thought to question the capacity of business to meet any standards imposed efficiently and at minimal cost. Indeed, we believed that if business turned to the task of assuring product or worker safety or environmental wholesomeness with good will, those ends could be accomplished at negligible cost. This faith, too, was not without

12. Yankelovich, *New Rules: Search for Self-Fulfillment in a World Turned Upside Down* (New York: Random House, 1981), p. 173.

substance, for it had more often than not proved true that when industry predicted that dire economic consequences would flow from proposed regulation, it nonetheless demonstrated innovativeness and efficiency in responding. A case in point is that of seat belts for automobiles. Faced with a legislative proposal in the early 1960s that seat belt installation be mandated in all new vehicles, witnesses for the automobile manufacturers solemnly warned that compulsory installation would add substantial unwanted costs to each vehicle. Implemented as standard equipment, the installed costs to the buyer dropped by two-thirds in five years—about ten dollars a pair.[13]

While confidence in business's capacity to perform persisted, as Wilson observes, "the perceived legitimacy of business enterprise declined."[14] Reaching back to the early nineteenth century is a strong strain of antipathy to the increasing massiveness, remoteness, and concentration of business enterprise, while no comparable antipathy had yet emerged with regard to the size or remoteness of the federal government. Corporate repute was further undermined by a series of scandals, extending from the General Electric price-fixing criminal convictions in the late 1950s to the exploitive drug-pricing and thalidomide shocks dramatically illuminated by Estes Kefauver in the early 1960s. The cigarette industry, for example, contributed generously to growing public skepticism as to the morality of business. Its seductive marketing themes, often targeted on young people through ubiquitous television commercials, flouted the moral implications of the conclusive evidence that its products were killing hundreds of thousands of Americans prematurely. Thus, while some industries' moral myopia contributed to skepticism about business's social responsibility, business's technical performance reaffirmed our faith in its capacity.

As Wilson observes, "Entrepreneurial politics depends heavily on the attitudes of third parties: political elites; media; influential writers; committee staffs; heads of voluntary associations; political activists" (to which he might well have added academics).[15] The prevailing liberal tenets were virtually unchallenged. Conservatism marked the political deviate. The Young Americans For Freedom,

13. Ralph Nader, *Unsafe at Any Speed: The Designed-in Dangers of the American Automobile* (New York: Grossman, 1965), pp. 121, 128.
14. Wilson, *The Politics of Regulation*, p. 365.
15. Ibid., p. 371.

for example, where not dismissed as a lunatic fringe, were consigned to a discredited older generation as "young fogies."

In 1964 the political tides were propitious. Lyndon Johnson had not only won a decisive victory over Barry Goldwater, but had brought in with him perhaps the most liberal Congress in history. Conservatives still held tightly to key levers of Congress, such as the chairmanships of the Rules Committee in the House and the Judiciary Committee in the Senate, but they were perceived, and perceived themselves to be, on the political and ideological defensive.

By the mid-1960s, liberals in Congress, especially the Senate class of 1958, had begun to rise, through seniority and attrition, to committee chairmanships and positions of party influence, while the democratization of the Senate under Majority Leader Mansfield dispersed power more broadly than ever among the liberal majority of Senate Democrats. Simply to call the roll of Senate liberals serves to recall the sense of the beckoning ascendancy of liberalism: Kefauver, Hart, Humphrey, Gore, Morse, Muskie, Douglas, Clark, Ribicoff, Proxmire, Nelson, Yarborough, McGovern, McCarthy, Magnuson, Jackson, Kennedy—and, on the Republican side, Javits, Percy, Aiken, Cooper, Case, Brooke.

The stirrings of student and dissident reaction against perceived adventurism in Vietnam fueled a growing tendency among opinion leaders to question previously unchallenged institutions, including the multinational corporations.

Organized labor was perceived as the strongest organized political constituency, the predominant institutional source of campaign financing. With wages and working conditions largely secure, labor leadership could turn confidently to the pursuit of social welfare and consumer issues.

In the public political arena, business was quiescent—and defensive. Except for those industries that nestled comfortably in the protective shade of quota, tariff, or economic regulation, most American business, relatively undisturbed by Washington and flourishing, gave low priority to national political involvement.

Indeed, liberal ideas had set the national agenda to such an extent that many businessmen were themselves deeply troubled by the issues raised by consumer advocates (and by their own children). John Wheeler, for many years the principal Washington lobbyist for Sears Roebuck and Co., became convinced while recuperating from a heart attack that Sears must pursue a course of corporate statesmanship. He successfully convinced Sears management to support federal product-safety and warranty legislation publicly.

Though it now appears at least mildly astonishing, in 1966 Ralph Nader was named one of the Junior Chamber of Commerce's outstanding young men. In 1973 the new president of the National Chamber of Commerce itself, the president of the State Farm Insurance Company, Edward B. Rust, declared, "Business should be grateful for Ralph Nader. He is single-mindedly committed to making the free-enterprise system work as it's supposed to—to making marketplace realities of the very virtues that businessmen ascribe to the system."[16] By 1967 the Chamber of Commerce had formed a committee on consumer interests, many of whose members were genuinely committed to exploring ways in which it could take the lead in affirmative initiatives responding to areas of concern raised by consumer advocates.

When, in Elizabeth Drew's felicitous term, the automobile industry had proved itself "a paper hippopotamus"[17] in failing to suppress safety legislation, an executive lamented, "One of the serious problems in our industry is provinciality. The auto industry is a giant, with a fantastic impact on the economy, but the sun rises in Detroit and sets in Dearborn. Besides, our laissez faire attitude had worked so far."[18]

The Bobby Baker scandal, which partly exposed and partly threatened to expose the pervasive illicit cash economy of the House and Senate, provoked demands for campaign-financing reform and enhanced congressional fear of exposure and attack by Drew Pearson and others as "tools of the special interests."

Businessmen, to an extent that now seems hardly credible, ignored Washington. In *The Corporation in American Politics* (1969), Edwin Epstein documents the institutional, even social inhibitions against corporate involvement in national political affairs.[19] The "dirty work" of lobbying was best left to trade associations. Yet these organizations, especially the major umbrella groups, such as the Chamber of Commerce and the National Association of Manufacturers, were decaying, vestigial ornaments of the early twentieth

16. Rust, Speech before National Association of Life Insurance Underwriters Convention, Chicago, Ill., September 18, 1973.
17. Drew, "The Politics of Auto Safety," *Atlantic Monthly*, October 1965, p. 96.
18. Ibid., p. 98.
19. Epstein, *The Corporation in American Politics* (Englewood Cliffs, N.J.: Prentice-Hall, 1969).

century, neglected and scorned even among business leaders. While young public-interest volunteers worked well into the night, spurred by conviction and a sense of political momentum (if not manifest destiny), the business lobbyist, on the defensive, challenged in his good faith by his own children, earned his pay and reserved his commitment for the fifth hole at the congressional country club. And if the trade association failed to defeat some new regulatory scheme, that was hardly the end of the world, since in prosperous and buoyant markets, the cost of regulation could be passed on to consumers without risk.

Many Washington business lobbyists were themselves drawn from the ranks of former Democratic members of Congress and their staffs, which was only natural, since both houses of Congress had been dominated by the Democrats since 1954. While they facilely learned to place their client or employer's interest first, they themselves retained strong vestiges of the predominant liberal ethos. Personally, as they often told us, they identified with all our consumer initiatives save those that unfairly afflicted their clients. Many of the same lobbyists also harbored a self-interested need to maintain the status of incumbent Democrats in whom they had invested both personally and financially over the years, and were hence uninterested in building a successful Republican opposition, no matter how business-oriented. To the extent that they became involved in national political campaigns, most businessmen remained diffident. They were far more likely to direct their contributions to courting access to incumbents than to defeating them.

Why were consumer issues, in particular, ripe for exploitation by alert political entrepreneurs and for elevation to the national political agenda? Perhaps with rhetorical redundancy, I once concluded a draft speech for Senator Magnuson on the Commerce Committee's consumer agenda with a peroration decrying the "gaping gaps" in the fabric of the nation's consumer protection laws. The last major consumer protection law enacted before the Kefauver-Harris drug amendments in 1962[20] was the Food, Drug and Cosmetic Act of 1938.[21]

Perhaps automobiles and cigarettes most graphically exemplified these gaps. In a seminal piece published in the *New York Times Magazine* in 1964, Daniel Patrick Moynihan, then assistant secretary

20. Kefauver Act, Pub. L. No. 87–781, 76 Stat. 780 (1962).
21. Food, Drug, and Cosmetic Act, ch. 675, 52 Stat. 1040 (1938).

of labor (and the employer of a young auto-safety researcher named Ralph Nader) delineated the unreckoned toll taken by the automobile in death and debilitation and its drain upon the health care delivery system, the urban blight attributable to highway sprawl and the flight to the suburbs, the automobile's contribution to air pollution, and such secondary impacts as the burdening of the courts and the preoccupation of American lawyers with negotiating prices for ruined arms and legs.[22] Auto fatalities had risen to 50,000 per year by 1965, when General Motors president James Roach testified that his company, with 1.7 billion dollars in profits in 1964, had spent 1 million dollars on safety research.[23]

As for cigarettes, they had, as a category, miraculously (perhaps) escaped the jurisdiction of the Food and Drug Administration, qualifying neither as food, drug, nor cosmetic. Yet in 1962 the medical/ scientific community was presented with the authoritatively damning report of the British Royal College of Physicians, drawing a clear causal relationship between cigarette smoking and lung cancer.[24]

In the explosive growth of the U.S. economy since the Second World War, increasingly sophisticated products were being manufactured and distributed through national distribution systems, which consumers perceived as increasingly remote, unresponsive to consumer complaint, and inaccessible to local redress. There was a growing perception that U.S. product-quality standards had depreciated—though it may well have been that having for the first time acquired those goods for which they had worked and saved and dreamed, Americans had unrealistically high expectations. Certainly, complaints over new automobile failures and warranty malperformance abounded. Everyone had his woeful tale of an unredeemable "lemon." Increasingly sophisticated techniques for measuring latent product hazards were beginning to bring new issues to the surface, such as the epidemiological techniques that identified cigarette smoking's etiological role in lung disease and mild carcinogens in many common foods and drugs that had hitherto gone undetected.

22. Moynihan, "Next: A New Auto Insurance Policy," *New York Times Magazine*, August 27, 1967.
23. Drew "Politics of Auto Safety," p. 97.
24. Royal College of Physicians of London, *Smoking and Health* (New York, Pitman Publishing Corporation, 1962).

Other hazards (such as flammable cotton flannel sleepwear) and market malfunctions (such as inadequate and confusing food labeling on packaging) had not grown measurably worse. But the evolving social psychology of public "entitlement" (as Daniel Yankelovich has characterized it)[25] proved fertile ground for the evocation of public enthusiasm for proposed federal consumer remedies. When candidate John F. Kennedy delivered his "consumer" campaign speech in 1960, he was greeted with an exuberant enthusiasm that far exceeded his expectations.[26] It is easy to understand why, as president, he enlisted the efforts of a sturdy labor leader and consumer advocate, Esther Peterson, to draft the first presidential consumer message. This message, sent to Congress on March 15, 1962 spelled out a consumer bill of rights (the right to know, to be safe, to choose, and to be heard) and a (modest) agenda of consumer bills.[27] Opinion polls showed broad, though not necessarily deep, public endorsement of these and other consumer protection initiatives, as they do today.

By 1966 Johnson and the eighty-ninth Congress had neared completion of the broad liberal agenda carried over from the Eisenhower and early Kennedy years. In 1966 and 1967, as the costs of the war in Vietnam began to place an inflationary strain upon the U.S. economy and on the federal budget, consumer issues, which entailed little direct budgetary cost (as contrasted, for example, with poverty and housing programs) appealed increasingly to the president's agenda setters, such as Joseph Califano, domestic counsel in the White House. The contributions of the Chicago economists and the consequent deregulatory fervor were a decade away from reaching the national agenda. Regulatory reform meant ending the universally acknowledged capture of the regulatory agencies by the regulated. Business generally harbored little grievance at federal overregulation, since (save for industries that *chose* to be overregulated) most federal regulators had demonstrated exquisite sensitivity to industry's concerns.

25. *Report to Leadership Participants on 1980 Findings of Corporate Priorities* (New York: Yankelovich, Skelly, and White, 1980), p. 12.

26. U.S., Congress, Senate, Committee on Commerce, *Freedom of Communications*, S. Rept. 994, 87th Cong., 1st sess., 1961, *The Speeches, Remarks, Press Conferences and Statements of Senator John F. Kennedy, August 1 through November 7, 1959*, part 1, pp. 900–902.

27. U.S., President, *Public Papers of the President of the United States* (Washington, D.C.: Office of the *Federal Register*, National Archives and Records Service, 1953–), pp. 235–43.

The Democratic leaders of the Senate and House Commerce Committees were confident enough in the legitimacy of regulation as late as the fall of 1975 to express their concerns to President Ford over what they perceived as regulatory reform overkill. "Regulation," they wrote the president, "is as American as hot dogs, baseball, apple pie and Chevrolet."[28]

THE CONGRESSIONAL ENTREPRENEURS

Into this welcoming environment entered the entrepreneurs. It is no wonder that politicians were drawn to consumer advocacy. Consumer issues were homey, usually simple in conception, and of broad general interest. Perhaps most important, issues such as the safety of products like cigarettes, automobiles, and flammable fabrics lent themselves readily to the evocation of broad public outrage (e.g., burned and scarred infants, death by impalement on spearlike steering columns).

Politicians found they could market consumer issues through the media to voters in the political marketplace and sell themselves as advocates of attitudes and initiatives that a broad public constituency would buy. *They* really fit Wilson's marketplace image of the "entrepreneur" more tidily than public-interest advocates such as Ralph Nader (who might be considered "not-for-profit" entrepreneurs). Estes Kefauver, as chairman of the Senate antitrust and monopoly subcommittee, demonstrated in the 1950s how a full-throated attack on the steel, drug, and auto industries could further the ambition for the presidential nomination of a populist senator without a major urban state platform.

After Kefauver's death in 1963, Senator Philip Hart became chairman of the antitrust and monopoly subcommittee, laying the painstaking foundations of investigations and hearings that were to lead ultimately to passing the Fair Packaging and Labeling Act. At the same time, Paul Douglas on the Senate Banking Committee patiently pursued "truth-in-lending" legislation that William Proxmire was to guide to passage after Douglas's death. By mid-1964 Senator Gaylord Nelson had introduced a federal tire-safety bill,

28. "Congressional Democratic Policy Statement on Regulatory Reform," paper presented to the White House, mimeographed, June 25, 1975.

and by mid-February 1965, Senator Abraham Ribicoff would launch his chairmanship of the Senate Government Operations Committee's subcommittee on executive reorganization with hearings aimed at curbing "the fantastic carnage" on the nation's highways. In the states, young attorneys general such as Walter Mondale were emerging as formidable challengers for higher office on a political foundation of consumer advocacy and law enforcement.

Though barely more than a decade ago, it now seems strange indeed to us that Lyndon Johnson and other lawmakers sought to measure their effectiveness—and be measured—by the numbers of new laws proposed and enacted under their sponsorship. Indeed, much of the political energy behind many of the consumer initiatives was reinforced, if not generated, by lively competition for credit as the progenitor of consumer laws.

In no arena was this competition more heated and its results more palpable than in the pursuit of auto-safety legislation. Congressman Kenneth Roberts of Alabama stood alone on the issue for nearly a decade; then Senators Gaylord Nelson and Abraham Ribicoff, joined by Magnuson, then Senator Vance Hartke, and, finally, Congressman Harley Staggers, emerging as the new chairman of what had been a defiantly anti-consumer House Commerce Committee, supported the legislation. They were followed by Congressmen John Moss and Robert Eckhart, on the House committee, and later joined by Senator Frank Moss, following the 1968 election, as second chairman of the Senate's consumer subcommittee. Each competed boisterously for credit as either the author of legislation or the strongest advocate of auto safety. And all of them had to contend with Lyndon Johnson, who entered the lists with the administration's exceedingly modest auto-safety bill early in 1966. All combined in what Elizabeth Drew in the *Atlantic Monthly* labeled the "political car-safety derby."[29]

Consumer advocates in Congress, such as Maurine Neuberger, who had "taken on" the cigarette industry, were singled out for rare praise by muckrakers like Drew Pearson for their heroism in challenging the "special interests." Indeed, they could bask in the sunlight of public approval, while political retribution from business appeared remote.

---

29. Drew, "Politics of Auto Safety," p. 96.

THE ENTREPRENEURIAL COALITION

Though elected officials may be the purest of political entrepreneurs (and electoral politics their marketplace), their marketing of consumer political goods falls far short of explaining the peculiar nature of the surge in consumer legislation of the 1960s and early 1970s.

Not only were unprecedented numbers of consumer laws enacted during those years, but the customary congressional pattern of handling producer/consumer disputes was very nearly stood on its head. There had, after all, been earlier congressional entrepreneurs claiming credit for such laws as the first Flammable Fabrics Act or the Hazardous Substances Labeling Act of 1960[30] (which allowed warning labels, but *not* the banning of toxic cleaning fluids such as carbon tetrachloride, subsequently banned by the Consumer Product Safety Commission).

Typically in the past, a senator or congressman or responsible agency would have responded to a consumer scandal or crisis by drafting and introducing a bill minimally adequate to vent public outrage. Where the initiative had come from an agency accustomed to regulating an industry or from the appropriate committee chairmen, such legislation (as in the case of the first Flammable Fabrics Act) was often the product of extensive preintroduction negotiation. If not, as the bill wound its way through the tortuous succession of veto points called the legislative process, an alerted industry, employing one or another available legislative lever, would take care to assure that objectionable provisions melted away.[31] Since few constituents were prepared to analyze or follow the terms or implementation of such legislation, the congressional author's political purpose was achieved simply by claiming credit for the passage of a law bearing an impressive title.

By contrast, the auto-safety law and others that followed, like the Consumer Product Safety Act and the Magnuson-Moss Warranty and FTC Improvements Act, were drafted and introduced as comprehensive regulatory schemes and maintained essentially intact, if not strengthened, in their legislative passage. This unique throttling of business's accustomed access to, and influence on, the legislative

30. Hazardous Substances Act, Pub. L. No. 86–613, 74 Stat. 372 (1960).
31. For example, during the House Commerce Committee's consideration of the Fair Packaging and Labeling Act passed by the Senate, it eliminated the critical Senate provision authorizing mandatory standard sizes for grocery products to promote competition through comparison shopping.

process could only have taken place because of the simultaneous emergence of five distinct groups of entrepreneurs, who formed a tenuously organized, but mutually reinforcing and sustained, coalition:

1. Consumer advocates among senators and House members;

2. A new, or newly flourishing, strain of entrepreneurial congressional staff;

3. A newly aggressive core of investigative and advocacy journalists, who shared the advocates' view of consumer initiatives as moral imperatives;

4. Labor; and

5. The private not-for-profit issue entrepreneurs, such as Dr. Abe Bergman, but preeminently Ralph Nader—so much so that to him belongs primary credit for the persistent substantive and procedural strength, if not the very existence, of the major new consumer laws.

We'll examine representatives of each element of this coalition. First, let me turn to my own leader, Warren Magnuson, chairman of the Senate Commerce Committee from 1956 to 1977.

MAGNUSON AND THE SENATE
COMMERCE COMMITTEE

Observing Senator Magnuson in 1962, one might well not have marked him for future leadership as a consumer advocate. To be sure, shortly after his election to the Senate in 1946, he had expressed interest in heading an investigation of the life insurance industry as a joint venture with then Chairman Pat McCarran of the Judiciary Committee. (He wisely withdrew from the project when McCarran informed him that the investigation would have to be conducted without benefit of additional staff counsel and investigators.) And it was Magnuson, according to Richard Harris, the chronicler of the Kefauver-Harris drug reform law,[32] who first raised questions about the anti-competitive structure of prescription drug

32. Harris, *The Real Voice* (New York: Macmillan Co., 1964).

pricing at a congressional hearing (this time the FTC appropriations hearings in 1957).

Since 1956 Magnuson had chosen the primary role of defender and nurturer of Washington industries—the merchant marine and fisheries, aviation, and trucking. In his combined roles as chairman of the Commerce Committee and senior ranking member of the Appropriations Committee, he made certain that the state of Washington received ample allocations of federal expenditures. But, in the election of 1962, Magnuson experienced a rude shock. Previously a confident and skillful vote-gatherer, he came within 50,000 votes of losing his Senate seat to a political novice, a young Methodist minister who had never before run for political office. He brushed aside his old political cronies, soured by their hoary counsel and botched campaign, and turned for guidance and leadership to a brilliant young Yale and Harvard lawyer from the state of Washington, Gerald Grinstein, whose political acumen belied his Eastern academic gloss (perhaps because, himself the son of a Magnuson crony, he had observed and absorbed what was to be learned from Magnuson's early political experience, but escaped the older political generation's tendency to let that wisdom atrophy).

Having apprenticed, earning Magnuson's trust and respect as an assistant committee counsel handling the politically delicate merchant marine subcommittee, Grinstein's first order of business was to sweep the cobwebs from the Senate Commerce Committee, whose staff, it must be said, had not previously been celebrated for energy or initiative. He would rebuild with young professionals who met his standards both for professional excellence and political sensitivity.

I do not know when Magnuson and Grinstein determined that a strong pro-consumer record of achievement would be a major component of the political revitalization of Warren Magnuson, but in the fall of 1964, Grinstein, who had been a classmate of mine at Yale, asked me to join the staff of the Senate Commerce Committee in the newly created capacity of consumer counsel.

As a legislative assistant to Oregon Senator Maurine Neuberger, an early and enthusiastic consumer advocate, I had gained some experience and even more enthusiasm for the pursuit of consumer interests. I had assisted Senator Neuberger's efforts to launch an early challenge to the cigarette companies and, jointly with Senator Hart, to pursue packaging and labeling abuses. Grinstein promised a wider canvas in the Commerce Committee: a vastly more senior and powerful leader, Senator Magnuson, and an opportunity, through the creation of a new consumer subcommittee (which did not actually take place until 1976), to make a substantial contribution to consumer protection law.

My assignment: to help build a consumer record for Magnuson, to identify opportunities, develop strategies, shepherd bills, and make certain that Magnuson received appropriate acknowledgement for his achievements. Grinstein knew that I had been trained by Neuberger's administrative assistant, Lloyd Tupling (formerly a muckraking Northwestern journalist who had relished the private power controversies that occupied the stormy center of Northwestern politics for a generation). And he knew that the first lesson I had been taught as legislative assistant was never to write a speech, concoct an initiative, or draft a bill without simultaneously visualizing the press release.

For the next ten years, Grinstein and I gradually expanded the committee staff, absorbing a promising graduate of the University of Washington Law School each year, and building a corps of consumer legislation specialists through on-the-job training. By 1968 eight new consumer laws bore Magnuson's name as principal author.[33] And, in the campaign of 1968, Magnuson, who had never once mentioned consumer issues in his 1962 campaign, ran a series of striking newspaper and television ads. Across a full newspaper page in bold freehand appeared the following message trumpeting his consumer achievements:

There's a law that forced Detroit to make cars safer—Senator Magnuson's law.
There's a law that keeps the gas pipelines under your house from blowing up—Senator Magnuson's law.
There's a law that makes food labels tell the truth—Senator Magnuson's law.
Keep the big boys honest; let's keep Maggie in the Senate.

33. To promote highway safety, Pub. L. No. 88–466, 78 Stat. 564 (1964); Federal Cigarette and Labeling Advertising Act, Pub. L. No. 89–92, 79 Stat. 282 (1965); National Traffic and Motor Vehicle Safety Act of 1966, Pub. L. No. 89–563, 80 Stat. 718; Child Protection Act of 1966, Pub. L. No. 89–756, 80 Stat. 1303; to establish a national commission on product safety, Pub. L. No. 90–146, 81 Stat. 466 (1967); Flammable Fabrics Act Amendments, Pub. L. No. 90–189, 81 Stat. 568 (1967); Fire Research and Safety Act of 1968, Pub. L. No. 90–259, 82 Stat. 34; to establish a motor vehicle accident compensation system, Pub. L. No. 90–313, 82 Stat. 126 (1968).

Magnuson's consumer enterprise passed largely unremarked by political observers, with the exception of Jim Ridgeway, writing in *The New Republic* in 1966, who referred to Senator Magnuson in an ungenerous aside as busily changing his image from "corporate stooge" to consumer advocate.

THE ROLE OF STAFF

The second key component of the entrepreneurial coalition, sometimes deplored or feared, but only dimly perceived, were the congressional staffs. "Bumblebees," John Ehrlichman called us (to Magnuson's sardonic delight), hovering above the honey of power.

It is true that Magnuson's Commerce Committee never lacked for enthusiastic applicants, drawn, as Wilson observes, by the opportunity to pursue work perceived as both "morally correct" and "politically useful."

It is a measure of the ideological dominance of liberal values and remedies that the staff members drawn to the Commerce Committee could safely be selected by an independent faculty committee without regard to party affiliation or ideological commitment, though of course there was some measure of self-selection, as Magnuson became increasingly identified as a consumer advocate. Indeed, the staff member assigned principal responsibility for the Flammable Fabrics Act was Norman Maleng, who viewed himself, and subsequently pursued public office, as a staunch Republican.

In 1966 David Price, a graduate student in political science at Yale, pursued as his thesis the role of staff members on several Senate committees, most prominently the Commerce Committee. Comparing Magnuson's staff with the professionally competent, but defiantly neutral, staff of the Senate Appropriations Committee, Price labeled the latter "professional"; he called us "entrepreneurial," anticipating Wilson.[34]

The role of staff was critical, but it can be exaggerated. The lack of formal structure and poor visibility of the relationship between staff and legislators lends itself to demonology, such as the persistent myth that Magnuson's consumer efforts were the product of an

34. The Ralph Nader Congress Project, directed by David E. Price, *The Commerce Committees* (New York: Grossman Publishers, 1975), pp. 22–41.

unrestrained rogue staff. So persistent was this myth that, one day in late 1967, a former administrative assistant to Senator Magnuson, then a lobbyist for a major trade association, paid a visit to Magnuson at his home on behalf of old Magnuson hands in Washington's lobbying community. The purpose of the visit, said the old friend, was to bring to Magnuson's attention the (of course, selfless) concern among Magnuson's friends that, in his name and without his knowledge, Magnuson's overzealous staff were committing excesses in the name of consumer protection. Magnuson listened, nodded, and smiled. His friend was not reassured. Magnuson, it turned out, knew far more of the thrust and detail of his staff's activities than his friends had imagined. And it was quite clear that he held his staff in harmonious harness. Indeed, it had served his purpose to let his staff be cast as rogue zealots, with Magnuson their captive. That image conveyed the message to lobbyists that direct appeals to Magnuson for legislative clemency would be of little avail, so he spared himself the pain of denying the entreaties of old friends.

There were, indeed, sharply circumscribed limits to staff initiatives, but the role of the staff was undeniably critical. Foremost, the staff served as a professional resource, counterbalancing the extraordinary breath of legal and technical talent available to business. The crafting of effecting regulatory schemes is an arcane art, and the difference between effective and token regulation may well turn on the artful shaping of apparently innocuous and routine legislative boilerplate.

Staff also served as a source of psychic energy, buttressing and absorbing the stress of conflicting technical arguments for harrassed and burdened congressmen and senators. The relationship between senators or congressmen and their staffs is ambiguous and often emotionally complex. Unlike the structured hierarchies of government and business bureaucracies, the congressional office or committee more nearly resembles a petty Renaissance court, with power and advancement largely dependent on the temper of the relationship between principal and servant. These relationships are often intense mixtures of mutual respect and antagonism. Unhappily, however, staff are not infrequently seized with unearned self-importance, and grow arrogant and contemptuous of their own principal; while legislators are often uncommonly vain and jealous of their own staff's skills and knowledge.

But these relationships can also be enormously productive. Magnuson deliberately surrounded himself with staff much younger than himself. He drew energy from their enthusiasm. He gave them creative space, but only when he had satisfied himself that their judgment was reliable and harmonized with his own political philosophy and style. They, in turn, to gain respect and affection for their leader, had only to watch him subtly take charge and direct the temper and thrust of a contentious Senate-House Conference Committee to achieve his goals.

For many legislators, especially older members, whose social lives were spent mostly in the company of businessmen, lobbyists, and other worthies of the economic and political establishment, business perspective and influence were counterbalanced by their younger staffs, more attuned to the newer political generation— which in the 1960s meant less ambiguously liberal and more skeptical of institutions, especially of business, but not yet of government.

Even at the zenith of the consumer thrust in Congress, business lobbyists spoke powerfully for the various economic and political establishments. They were much of the bedrock of the political constituencies; for the most part they formed the elected officials' social and economic peer group; they represented the primary source, other than labor, of campaign funds.

But staff were constantly present. In the midst of the Senate Commerce Committee deliberations on auto safety, Rod Markely, then Washington vice-president of Ford and perhaps the most able representative of an auto manufacturer, called his neighbor Magnuson at home one evening to ask if he might drive the chairman to the office the next day. Markely had spent his career patiently ingratiating himself so that he could be in position to ask to drive Magnuson to the office, a priceless opportunity to talk alone. Magnuson declined. But within our staff, those who needed access to the chairman each morning seized the opportunity to drive him in.

Of one senior congressman, whose political renaissance through consumer advocacy was stimulated by a close and affectionate relationship with a lively and committed staff, an old friend observed, "They have power over him, because he sees, in their idealism, himself as a young man—or what he would like to think he was or might have been." Thus, it was in the *combination* of elected members and their staffs that one found the felicitous confluence of the consumer enterprise.

THE NOT-FOR-PROFIT CONSUMER ENTREPRENEURS

The third component of the consumer coalition was made up of private citizens, commonly labeled either "public-interest advocates" or "so-called public-interest advocates," according to one's political preferences. Though individual advocates like Nader stand out most vividly, it is important to emphasize that consumer advocacy in the late sixties and the seventies was not without substantial institutional underpinnings, especially organized labor. To the extent that consumer interests were advanced through the use of traditional political "clout," the unions supplied it. Their veteran lobbyists, wise in the folkways of Congress, enjoyed close, seasoned relationships with members and represented *organized* constituencies. These men and women entered the lists on behalf of most of the consumer bills, and they did so with a spirit of personal commitment beyond institutional endorsement.

Labor's involvement was hardly surprising, since the consumer movement of the 1930s had been closely intertwined with the rise of the labor movement. Indeed, this connection was symbolized by President Kennedy's assignment of a dual role to Esther Peterson, herself a legendary former organizer for the International Ladies Garment Workers Union, as assistant secretary of labor and special assistant to the president for consumer affairs. For many of the labor representatives, the fight for consumer legislation gave vent to an idealism mature unionism otherwise no longer engaged.

Labor, of course, had limiting, sometimes conflicting, goals. The unions' traditional approach and long-standing relationship with Congress sometimes clashed with the confrontational tactics of the new consumer advocates. But on most key consumer issues, labor lobbyists were there in force, cornering senators and congressmen and communicating their position in the familiar shorthand that only long-term, comfortable relationships support—a traditional political resource that dwarfed the efforts of all other consumer advocates combined.

Though I have preferred the term "consumer impulse" to "consumer movement," the successful effort in 1968 to bring together labor and other national and local consumer organizations in an umbrella coalition, the Consumer Federation of America, did demonstrate the breadth of the appeal of consumer issues to a broad constituency. As a loose coalition of organizations, however, CFA might well have lacked significant independent political presence were it not for the extraordinary skill and energy of its leadership—perhaps most forcefully, Carol Foreman, its executive director from 1973 to 1977.

During the late 1960s and early 1970s, the Nixon years, Foreman and Joan Claybrook, organizer, manager, and chief lobbyist of Congress Watch, Nader's "citizens' lobby," demonstrated the remarkable capacity of a handful of skilled and dedicated advocates to affect legislative decision making, with little more than zeal for political combat, a subtle sense of congressional motivation, and monumental determination and patience.

As the most venerable of consumer organizations, with more than a million members (though most may have viewed themselves primarily as subscribers to *Consumer Reports*), Consumer's Union took some time to shed its institutional diffidence concerning public advocacy, but became increasingly active in representing the consumer interest before Congress. And when it did, it conveyed the legitimacy of its tradition, the weight of its numbers, and its institutional expertise and recognition.

Then there were the individual advocates. Some, like Dr. Bergman, pursued their cause directly with responsive senators and congressmen and their staffs. Others, such as Jessica Mitford, whose exposés of abuses in funeral practices led indirectly to a Federal Trade Commission investigation,[35] could trace their lineage to the progressive muckrakers.

And then there was Ralph Nader. How does one begin to take his measure? Like Mitford or Lincoln Steffens, a painstaking chronicler of public and corporate malfeasance: a muckraker. But, unlike the investigative journalist, whose task ends with exposé, Nader was also a scourge of the regulatory process—of the historic breakdown between legislative promise and effective implementation.

More than an investigator and scholar, drawing upon, but transcending, his lawyer's skills, he was an advocate skilled at seizing the symbols of debate—not a traditional advocate but one finely attuned to the uses and the needs of the media: the beats, the deadlines, the need for fresh "copy," for conflict, for heroism if available, but certainly for villainy, and, above all, for clarity and simplicity. ("Ralph Nader speaks in perfect bites!" said a TV consumer reporter, with professional respect.)

35. Mitford, *The American Way of Death* (New York: Simon & Schuster, 1963).

But even these significant roles diminish his contribution. For a very broad segment of the U.S. public, his has been the voice and persona of a contemporary Old Testament prophet: not a political radical, but, like the prophets, deeply conservative, calling society to account for its drift from its own professed morality. To people troubled by the "cultural contradictions of capitalism" (in Daniel Bell's phrase),[36] Nader evoked the neglected ethic of community responsibility.

He called the business community to account for its abandonment of the puritan ethic of "right livelihood," and he called government to account for its failure to respond to the will and needs of the Democratic majority rather than the economically privileged, invoking the morality of social responsibility and accountability. He was lively, but not ingratiating. He would not abide the conventions of politics. He was intemperate and prickly; he attacked allies; he would rather compromise too late than too early. His work was his leisure; his social life satisfying only to the extent that it furthered his causes. He could be witty, but his wit, too, drew upon the wellsprings of his indignation.

For those already enlisted in the consumer cause, he was the drill sergeant. He roused us from sleep and relaxation and plagued us into the night. He goaded, scolded, and teased. There was warmth and affection, too, but it was not readily forthcoming. Praise was rare, and, when granted, it was invariably qualified by expectation of future surpassing deeds. He understood that if the energy behind consumer initiatives flagged, if the attention of senators and congressmen was allowed to be diverted, if they became worn down and enervated by conflict, business, politically and institutionally resourceful, would ultimately persevere.

I first met Ralph Nader in the summer of 1965. We met over coffee (at least, I had coffee) in the Senate staff cafeteria. I had been assigned as the staff member responsible for tire-safety legislation, on which the Commerce Committee had been holding hearings. It was about six months before publication of *Unsafe at Any Speed,* and eight months before the public revelation of General Motors' investigative efforts to intimidate Nader, or at least unearth his vulnerabilities.[37]

36. Bell, *The Cultural Contradictions of Capitalism* (New York: Basic Books, 1976).
37. For a detailed account of this episode, see Thomas Whiteside, *The Investigation of Ralph Nader: General Motors vs. One Determined Man* (New York: Arbor House, 1972).

With barely contained fury, he delineated for me the sub-industries that had evolved with an economic stake in the continued high level of automobile accidents—and injuries: the auto repair shops, the personal injury lawyers, the wreckers and salvage yards; even the surgeons and emergency rooms. But, above all, the auto companies. With their economic stake in the extremely profitable market for crash parts, the automobile industry, he maintained, had no economic incentive to improve the crashworthiness of new cars—and would not do so until compelled by federal regulation. I was sympathetic (but uncomfortable at the unaccustomed passion of his conviction).

I expressed sympathy for his case, but with all the sophistication of a three-year Senate staff veteran, proceeded to lecture him on the realities of the legislative process. Despite Magnuson's consumer commitment, the Senate Commerce Committee remained a conservative institution. I could not conceive of its members participating in a comprehensive legislative assault upon so powerful a political citadel as the U.S. automobile industry. He was disappointed in my response, but undeterred. I was, of course, wrong. He was by that next January—and again and again—to extend our horizon of the legislatively possible.

Finally, Nader proved to be a skilled and resourceful political strategist. He understood that the political energy needed to offset the privileged position of business had to be generated through the media by broad and sustained public outrage, perceived by Congress as a potential source of political retribution if they failed adequately to address the sources of that outrage. To a citizenry coming increasingly to despair of the *possibility* of government responsiveness to the individual, Nader's appeal also lay in his refusal to give up on the American promise that democratic government could be responsive to the demands and needs of the ordinary citizen—a symbol of the potential capacity of Everyman to affect political change.

Nader's appeal also lay in conveying to the citizen a sense of efficacy, by demonstrating that an unconnected citizen—neither part of the establishment nor enjoying a formal position of power or prestige—could effect change. For a skeptical society, he became a symbol of trustworthiness. To a society losing faith in the capacity of ordinary citizens to shape their lives, he held out the hope of responsive government.

Nader has sustained his status as a public figure without institutional standing with only modest diminution for almost twenty years. For this sustained celebrity, one can look partly to his clarity and skill in communicating with a broad public, his sense of the dramatic, and a flair for the vital, fresh image and example. But Nader has also taken care to conserve his public identity. He deliberately avoided engaging in such deeply divisive public issues as the Vietnam war, at least in part so that he could husband the resource of his identity and uniqueness as a consumer advocate.

Nader understood the liberal journalist's self-image; appealing to their pride in the importance of their mission, conveying the sense that journalistic courage and the truth (including brand names) could be the antidote in a democratic society to unaccountable government and corporate power. Though business critics tend to view Nader as "the great regulator," he succeeded partly because much of his message constituted an attack upon the lethargy and inadequacy of regulators. In associating himself with the consumer's pain and frustration, not with more or oppressive government regulation, it remains his skill, especially in his appearances on national television, to be able to relate to, to resonate with the frustrations and anger of the ordinary citizen. As Tony Schwartz, the preeminent political media consultant, has written, the successful political candidate is not the one who spells out specific solutions to problems, but the one who convinces his constituency that he shares their concerns.[38] When the consumer gets stuck with a lemon of a new car, he may say, "There ought to be a law!" But he is even more likely to ask, "Where is Ralph Nader when I need him?"

THE MEDIA

Though their inclusion as a part of the consumer entrepreneurial coalition was implicit, never explicit, no consumer political enterprise would have been possible without responsive media. Wilson attributes the success of the consumer entrepreneurs to their activating in the press what he believes is a narrow subspecies of journalist, "those who bring an anti-business attitude to their jobs." That's both too narrow and mean spirited. I discovered during my years as a staff member on the Senate Commerce Committee that I could safely *assume* that virtually *any* national reporter assigned to

38. Tony Schwartz, *The Responsive Cord* (Garden City, N.Y.: Anchor Press, 1973).

cover the story of some piece of consumer legislation or other would be unabashedly sympathetic with the aims of the legislation, though they were hardly all consumed with anti-business animus. I unhesitatingly took into my confidence reporters with whom I had had no prior dealings, and I was rarely disappointed or embarrassed.

It is true that for certain publications, columnists provided the most receptive forums for advancing consumer initiatives and spotlighting business lobbying efforts to thwart those initiatives. Drew Pearson and, later, Jack Anderson and his associate Les Whitten were perhaps the most feared and, hence, the most potent journalistic guardians against what they perceived and characterized as subversion of congress by special interests.

I remember with a perhaps perverse fondness my first encounter with Drew Pearson. It was in 1965, when I was an exceedingly tentative staff member assigned to my first major consumer bill, the Hart-Magnuson fair packaging and labeling bill. The committee had been meeting in (then) closed-door executive session, and Magnuson had encountered unaccustomed resistance among committee members, who had been hearing from a well-organized consortium of food manufacturers, organized and led by Procter & Gamble's Bryce Harlow. No more than an hour after the executive session, I received a call from Magnuson, my first, with an order to come to his office forthwith. There, sitting across the table from him, was the fabled Drew Pearson.

"Tell Drew what went on in the executive session," said the chairman.

I proceeded to spell out the character and source of advocacy of the food manufacturers' position within the committee. I reported the sage counsel of Tennessee Senator Ross Bass, who, in response to the information that potato chips were packaged in more than sixty odd weights and sizes under a pound, thereby making it virtually impossible for a prudent housewife to choose the least expensive by unit measure, had responded, "Any woman who feeds her children potato chips isn't worth protecting!" When I was finished, Magnuson dismissed me. Pearson stayed.

Five days later, in his "Washington Merry-Go-Round" column, an anonymous inside source was credited with revelations on the attempt by named members of the Senate Commerce Committee to deprive the consumer of honest labeling and fair packaging in consumer products. The next day, the committee met once again to complete its work on the bill. In accordance with what was then already a vain ritual, one of the members thus publicly embarrassed demanded of the chairman an investigation of "leaks" from the committee. Magnuson nodded gravely at this lamentable breach of the committee's sanctity. He looked piercingly around the room at the outer rim of staff members. I sat as impassively as I knew how. "Have any of you staff members been talking to the press—been talking to Drew Pearson?" No head moved. Magnuson waited. The room was still. Magnuson frowned. Then, he abruptly turned to the agenda and within an hour the packaging and labeling bill, substantially intact, was on its way to the floor of the Senate.

Pearson/Anderson's willingness—indeed delight—in publishing ad hominem revelations of congressional backsliding in their syndicated network of 1,100 papers made them a formidable political force. Nader's ability to ferret out from his congressional sympathizers details of off-stage lobbying, the investigative work of the "Nader's Raiders" unmasking bureaucratic malingering, combined with Nader's unslackening moral indignation, meshed perfectly with Anderson's philosophical predilections and journalistic needs.

The *Washington Post*, the one paper all congressmen and senators read each morning, was also graced with the consumer reporting of Morton Mintz, as indefatigable in the pursuit of consumer injury, bureaucratic inertia, and congressional obfuscation as Nader—a scrupulously exact reporter, but one who miraculously never became inured to the ethical sleights-of-hand endemic to official Washington, especially the Congress, a journalist whose threshold of outrage remained low and frequently breached.

Unlike Anderson/Whitten, Mintz was a reporter first, not an advocacy journalist. But he insisted upon covering hearings that would otherwise have quickly faded from sight, like the Flammable Fabrics hearings, and he fought his editors constantly for more space, not on the distant business pages but up front.

There was Herblock, the political cartoonist. Who could portray more venomously the illicit conspiracy of special interests and their congressional cohorts as cabals of corpulent, corrupt tycoons, malignantly arrayed against the frail, friendless consumer?

Consumer advocates also found sympathetic ear and voice in the *Post's* editorial board, which, drawing substance and nourishment from Mintz's reporting, returned again and again to argue unequivocally against weakening consumer bills.

Though Anderson and Mintz and the *Washington Post* were of critical importance, the mostly anonymous and generally unremarked congressional wire service reporters were only slightly less important, because of their enormous reach to every city and town in the country. Reporters such as Patrick Sloyan of UPI and Bill Mead of AP cared enough to devote stringently rationed paragraphs to the revelations of corporate misdeeds unfolding in hearings and congressional debate.

THE ENTERPRISE

Confronted with Senator Magnuson's proposed Flammable Fabrics Act amendments, a lobbyist for the cotton textile industry vowed, with flamboyant confidence born of the habit of influence, that blood would run in the halls of Congress before passage of the act.

In response to that challenge, we set about structuring the Commerce Committee hearings on the proposed bill with what I confess was a certain macabre relish. Our objective was simple: to gain access to the media, to evoke public concern and reaction to the pain and suffering caused by child burnings, and to demonstrate the failure of the industry to make any effort in good faith to raise the inadequate voluntary standards of flammability.[39]

As one of our first witnesses, we invited the new special assistant to the president for consumer affairs, Betty Furness, a celebrity whose lack of visible credentials had made her appointment controversial. Her maiden appearance before a committee of Congress would, we knew, be a significant media event, and would guarantee the presence of network cameras as well as wide attendance by other national media. She would be the door-opener to broad public attention.

---

39. Though we did, indeed, attempt to structure hearings for maximum drama, we did not, in my memory, ever attempt to deny a business group an opportunity to present its case for the record. (Though its witnesses might well appear after the nightly news camera crews had shot their quota of film and packed up for the day.)

We adhered to this principle, partly though our sense of fair play and partly because Senator Magnuson had taught us well that the denial of the opportunity to testify invariably created a diversionary issue for a business group. No matter how much delay ensued (and often that was the very motive of the request to testify, made at the eleventh hour), the committee leadership supporting legislation was always in a more commanding moral posture having afforded opponents their full day in court.

Furness was followed immediately by Peter Hackes, the prominent CBS news commentator. Several months earlier, reading of Senator Magnuson's concern over flammable fabrics, he had called to offer his suport, citing his own family's tragic experience in the burning of an eleven-year-old daughter, whose cotton blouse (which he had determined met all current standards) had exploded into flames after she accidentally dropped a match on it. We asked him if he would tell the story of his own family's pain and suffering and economic hardship—the story of a family with whom the senators and the public would readily identify.

Dr. Bergman, in his testimony, also managed to put in stark human terms the tragedies represented by the impersonal statistics on child burnings that other witnesses were to give. Speaking of the dozens of other young children he had seen hideously burned by flammable clothing, Berman went on to say: "In all honesty I must say that I do not consider it a triumph when the life of a severely burned child is saved. A lifetime of operations, pain, disfigurement, scarring, and rejection by society and self lie ahead. Death may be more merciful."[40]

The next day the cotton textile council had its opportunity to respond. It maintained that no new legislation was necessary, that the Flammable Fabrics Act had "done the job Congress intended it to do" and called its results "admirable."[41] It argued that no further legislation was necessary, for the industry, through its voluntary standards review committee, was hard at work to raise the standards as high as textile technology would economically permit.

"How often," asked Senator Magnuson, "does your standards committee meet?" "Regularly, Senator," responded the cotton council representative.

Indeed, it turned out that the industry's standards committee had—lately—been meeting regularly, but only after prompting by a letter Senator Magnuson had written to the secretary of commerce questioning the adequacy of the existing flammable fabrics standard. When, Magnuson asked, had the committee last met prior to that letter?

Ten years earlier.

40. U.S. Congress, Senate, Committee on Commerce, *Flammable Fabrics Act Amendments, Hearings before a Subcommittee of the Senate Committee on Commerce on S. 1003,* 90th Cong., 1st sess., 1967, p. 78.

41. Ibid., pp. 83–84.

MOTIVATING CONGRESS

I cannot say now that our tactics were coolly and deliberately calculated. They were perhaps as much the product of political instinct. It
is nonetheless evident, at least in retrospect, that they were played
out against an operational construct of congressional behavior that,
however unarticulated, served the consumer advocacy cause well.

At a basic level, our operational assumptions concerning the psychology of congressional behavior were mechanistic. We assumed
that congressional votes and related behavior involving consumer-
producer conflicts will ordinarily tend to support the producer,
given the normally high level of producers' political influence—
especially gratitude for past campaign contributions and the promise of future beneficence—unless there are substantial political costs
or risks entailed in so doing. Opposition by a prominent union was
one such cost. For most consumer issues, however, the greatest
potential cost lies in public notoriety: critical attention in the media
that potentially translates into an exploitable issue for a potential
political opponent and, ultimately, voter retribution at the next election.

But we also knew that members of Congress were not simply
political mechanisms. Emotions like greed, vanity, friendship, and
loyalty, of course, played a role in determining congressional behavior, not only in influencing votes but in shaping the determination and persistence with which a position, once taken, was pursued. The ability of the media to confer hero status upon those
perceived as fearlessly challenging "special interests" or championing the cause of the lone consumer, or who were singled out from
among "politicians" for the title of "statesman," could cast a lure to
snare even relatively conservative politicians.

Even members whose electoral status was secure and conservatives whose fundamental sympathies lay with the concerns of business recoiled from being labeled by Drew Pearson or Jack Anderson
as "tools of the special interests."[42] Many sought surcease from the
righteous wrath of their politically aroused, college-age children.
One need not embrace Marshall McLuhan's concept of the "global

42. In the 1960s it was, of course, not yet necessary to point out that a consumer, an
environmental, or civil rights concern was not what we meant by a "special interest."
"Special interest" meant simply moneyed interests—and not small moneyed interests, as in the case of the individual consumer, but big moneyed interests.

village"[43] to recognize, as Tony Schwartz has done, that the intimacy of the broadcast media can be as potent a vehicle for public shaming as the stocks in a prerevolutionary New England town.

Consumer strategists recognized other, perhaps more mundane, emotions as well. The truth is that most veteran congressmen and senators ardently seek to avoid controversy. It is a cliché that the upright legislator is one against whom equal pressures are applied from all directions. Otherwise the tendency is simply to give in to whichever pressures are unmatched by counterpressures. The stimulation by consumer advocates of public controversy makes it less tempting for the legislator simply to accede to the importuning of business representatives—if only because of the knowledge that in so doing one invites energy-draining conflict and confrontation, the spoiling of otherwise pleasant visits to one's district, and the agitation of the local media.

As staff members, we came to view our principals as a congeries of personal and political instincts and coexisting motivations ranging from the venal to the heroic. We understood that even the most zealous entrepreneurial staff member could frame issues in such a way as to resonate with the senator or congressman's more idealistic or populist instincts.

SECURING A PLACE ON THE NATIONAL
AGENDA: CHANNELING OUTRAGE

It was against this backdrop of perceived congressional motivations that strategies evolved. It was not enough simply to evoke concern over burnt children; it was necessary to channel that concern into public outrage at the failure of Congress to strengthen the flammable fabrics law. A critical part of that channeling process was the need to focus attention on the chosen legislative or regulatory instrument as the only legitimate response to a culpable business failure. That is one way in which a legislative initiative is placed upon the public agenda. Crucial to the process is legitimating the legislative initiative.

In the case of the flammable fabrics amendments, this was rela-

43. Marshall McLuhan and Quentin Fiore, *War and Peace in the Global Village* (New York: Bantam Books, 1968).

tively simple, since Congress had already enacted an earlier flammable fabrics law. The task was simply to prove it inadequate—and to show that industry's promise to remedy that inadequacy through voluntary action was empty. Note that part of the process of establishing the legitimacy of legislation may lie in undermining the legitimacy of voluntary industry response. As Wilson observes, the need for crisis or scandal is less acute for the political entrepreneur where the industry is not "associated in the popular mind with positive values."

In the case of automobile safety, Nader faced a more difficult task in legitimating federal regulatory legislation as the appropriate response to the highway death toll. Though there was, indeed, sufficient highway mayhem to constitute a national scandal, there had been no sudden nor dramatic escalation of the accident toll. Perhaps an even more serious inhibition was the prevailing public belief that automobile accidents were primarily the result of driver, rather than manufacturer, failure. As Nader argued, this public attitude had been carefully nurtured by the automobile industry for many years. The industry had furnished the primary financial support to the National Safety Council (which remained, perhaps not surprisingly, unenthusiastic about auto-safety legislation), generously underwriting its inexorable Labor Day body counts, its exhortations against drinking while driving, etc. All this was, of course, valid caution, but the constant focus on the driver also served to deflect public attention and concern from the design and safe construction of the vehicles themselves. Indeed the auto industry embraced a safety slogan that implicitly denied the role of the vehicle in automobile safety: "It's the nut behind the wheel." A General Motors vice-president for engineering, quoted in the *New York Times* in response to the agitation for federal safety standards, pleaded, "The driver is most important, we feel. If the drivers do everything they should, there wouldn't be accidents, would there?"[44]

The public tended to accept the highway death and injury toll as an inevitable cost of its chosen public transportation system. Indeed, it could still be said in the 1960s that the nation's deep emotional involvement with the automobile as a symbol of individuality and macho virility, stimulated by advertising imagery, had not waned. This imagery was antithetical to the antiseptic imagery of a transportation mode concerned with the safe packaging of its occu-

44. Drew, "Politics of Auto Safety," p. 95.

pants. In resisting safety proposals, auto industry spokesman played skillfully upon these images, protesting that "no one wants to drive a Sherman tank."

Through the publication of *Unsafe at Any Speed,* and his efficient exploitation of the David vs. Goliath appeal that flowed from the illicit General Motors investigation of him and the subsequent lawsuit, Nader gained access through the media to a broad public audience. He evoked the outrage of GM's deliberate disdain of safe design in the building of the Corvair. And, equally important, he introduced and nurtured the concept of "the second collision"—the concept that, while driver error or carelessness or bad luck may contribute to an accident, the life or death, mutilation or safety of the occupant is largely determined by the resulting collision of the passengers with the car's interior: the spearlike steering column, exposed knobs, and shattering glass. He argued that the safe or unsafe packaging of the automobile's occupants was a social responsibility of the manufacturer, which had been sorely neglected in the interest of cost. When the automobile industry responded that it was the consumer's right to buy automobiles of any design and charged Nader with impeding freedom of choice, Nader wryly responded that it was admirable of the industry to defend that cherished civil liberty, "the inalienable right to go through the windshield."[45]

NURTURING LEGITIMACY

We came to understand that success in overcoming business resistance lay as much in the careful cultivation and nurturing of the legitimacy of the laws proposed as in the political husbandry of public outrage. This learning process is well-illustrated by the strategies that led to the passage of the Consumer Product Safety Act and the creation of a new independent regulatory agency, the National Commission on Product Safety.

Shortly after passage of the automobile safety law, Senator Magnuson and his staff began to explore what seemed to be the next logical step, omnibus product-safety legislation covering other potentially hazardous manufactured consumer products. The Food and Drug Administration, without regulatory authority, had carried

45. Quoted in Connie Bruch, "Will Reaganism Revive Ralph Nader?" *American Lawyer*, May 1981, p. 28.

on an extremely modest program monitoring product-related injuries through a small and low-priority Office of Product Safety. This office had accumulated sketchy, but disturbing, evidence indicating that there might indeed be substantial public injury attributable to the faulty design and manufacture of a broad range of consumer products.

We decided that the concept of an independent national product-safety commission to regulate product safety, while needed and sound, was not politically ripe. The injuries attributable to such products were insufficiently documented and the public insufficiently alert to the extent of the risks to furnish a sufficient base of public support for immediate legislation. Moreover, the concept of a new regulatory commission lacked familiarity and legitimacy. So Senator Magnuson introduced legislation (in itself a legitimating step) to create a temporary National Commission on Product Safety to study the issue and hold hearings around the country, to develop a record of evidence on product hazards, to focus public attention, and to develop "appropriate recommendations."

It had been our experience that businesses tended to become politically aroused only when regulatory action was directly poised to regulate their behavior. A study commission looking to the possibility of future regulation would, therefore, generate little negative political energy on the part of business. Indeed, the study commission bill was introduced with the unaccustomed co-sponsorship of the conservative ranking Republican member of the Senate Commerce Committee, Norris Cotton, in early 1967, and was on the president's desk by the end of the same year. The only change sought by industry (the Association of Home Appliance Manufacturers) was a change in the proposed title of the commission from the "National Commission on Hazardous Household Products" to the "National Commission on Product Safety."

It was our expectation, of course, that the commission's deliberations would lead inexorably to a legislative proposal for the creation of a permanent consumer product safety commission, with full authority to set product safety standards and to order recalls. As anticipated, the commission's regional hearings developed a public record on such design shortcuts and flaws as baby cribs with slats spread so wide to save a few cents that they could catch the heads of infants and strangle them, and instant turn-on systems for television sets that spontaneously burst into flames. Since Morton Mintz sought, and was assigned by the *Washington Post*, to follow the commission from city to city, the hearings and revelations were assured not only of intense regional coverage and interest, but of a national (i.e., Washington, D.C.) audience as well.

By the time the commission issued its final report and delivered to Senator Magnuson and other congressional leaders draft legislation to create a permanent product-safety commission, public perception of the need for remedial legislation and the legitimacy of such a commission had been fully seeded.

OUTRAGE AS AN UMBRELLA

The strategy leading to the passage of the Magnuson-Moss Act to strengthen FTC rule-making powers, on the other hand, involved the political use of spontaneous public outrage. In 1969 the Senate Commerce Committee, as part of its interest in overseeing the performance of the Federal Trade Commission, had invited each of its sitting members to propose remedies to deficiencies in the commission's underlying authority, which, in their individual judgments, had contributed to the "Nader's Raiders" and the American Bar Association's assessment of the commission as not only spiritless, but toothless as well.[46]

The commissioners, warming eagerly to that task, outlined a series of proposed legislative reforms, from industrywide rule-making powers to enhanced FTC authority to obtain injunctions to halt deceptive advertising campaigns. This shopping list of FTC regulatory reforms was formidable but, to the leadership of the consumer subcommittee, Senators Magnuson and Moss, convincing. Yet, as structural and procedural reforms, they lacked the dramatic appeal of a flammable fabrics or product safety act.

At about the same time, the committee's attention had been drawn to legislative proposals to provide consumer relief from malperformance and exculpatory fine print in product warranties. No other single consumer complaint registered such widespread frustration and indignation. (Indeed, it had been my experience, in speaking with business groups in defense of consumer legislation,

46. Edward F. Cox, Robert L. Fellmeth, and John E. Schultz, *The Nader Report on the Federal Trade Commission* (New York: Grove Press, 1969); American Bar Association, "Report of the Commission to Study the Federal Trade Commission," September 15, 1969.

that one could readily deflect attention from their particular industry's complaint of overregulation to their own individual frustration with new car lemons, thereby evoking the latent consumerist even among the most conservative businessmen.)

To take advantage of the energy behind warranty reform, in the bill, which came to be known as the Magnuson-Moss Act, we married warranty reform (Title I of the act) to a series of FTC Act amendments drawn from the commissioners' prescriptions (Title II). Though many factors aided in the nurturing and passage of that legislation (including a virtuoso lobbying performance by Congress Watch and the Consumer Federation of America), the ease with which consumers (and senators) could relate to the warranty provisions of the bill and their genuine popularity provided critical legislative loft for the more significant, but emotionally unprepossessing, FTC reforms.

CONCLUSION

In those early days we saw ourselves as the Scarlet Pimpernels of the consumer movement: secret, or, in any event, unsung heroes doing good by doing in corporate abuse. One day during the late 1960s, I received a telephone call from former Kentucky Senator Earle Clements, then president of the Tobacco Institute. The day before, Senator Frank Moss, then chairman of the Commerce Committee's consumer subcommittee, had issued a bitter press release decrying the rise in expenditures for cigarette print advertising despite the congressionally mandated withdrawal of cigarette advertising from television, citing the "fact" that cigarette smoking caused the premature deaths of "300,000 Americans each year." Clements, not surprisingly, disputed the "fact." He assumed (correctly) that I had had a hand in drafting the Moss press release. His rebuke was mild, and characteristically defensive.

"You know, Pertschuk, when you're on the side of the angels, it's easier to stretch the truth."

Indeed, in those days we did see ourselves as on the side of the angels, and we were largely so perceived by the media and other reference groups that mattered. Nor were we immune from the curse of pride and the illusion of omnipotence that convinces each generation gaining political power that its successes are evidence of its own skills and virtue, and therefore fated to continue indefinitely.

Though we had hardly been able to achieve all that we proposed, we did not appreciate the uniquely benign political environment within which we had the good fortune to operate. We neither comprehended the severely circumscribed, inherent limits to our strategies, nor took adequate note of the lowering clouds of gathering business concern and mobilization.

2

The New PACs Americana:
Revitalization of Business Political Action

In December 1980, the late *Washington Star,* with uncommon gener-
osity, editorially commended the political maturity—if not the wisdom—of the Federal Trade Commission. While the staff of the commission had concluded that television advertising directed at young
children was inherently and pervasively deceptive, the staff con-
fessed—prudently said the *Star*—that it could conceive of no remedy for such deception. Hence the commission should close its rule-
making inquiry into children's advertising practices. At long last,
sighed the *Star,* the FTC was responding appropriately to the "public howl" against government regulation.[1]

This public howl is a curious phenomenon. Its decibel level is
indeed attested to by such sensitive polls as the Yankelovich survey
for *Time* magazine, taken in mid-May 1981, confirming that by a
two-to-one margin Americans want the government to "stop regulating business and protecting the consumer and let the free enterprise system work."[2]

"Howl" theorists such as the *Star's* editorial writer thus offer an
explanation for Washington's retreat from regulation that is congenial to both business sentiment and democratic theory: that deregulation is simply a response to the will of the people. But if we turn
our public hearing aids down a notch, we discover that the apparent

1. "The Kid-Vid Blunder" (editorial), *Washington Star,* April 19, 1981.
2. John F. Stacks, "It's Rightward On," *Time,* June 1, 1981, pp. 12–13.

howl is, instead, a far more subtle polyphony. While the public does, indeed, recoil from the *term* "regulation," it simultaneously displays a constant faith in the substance of whole categories of regulation.

Overwhelming majorities continue undaunted to support continued regulation of industrial safety, auto emissions and safety standards, and environmental restraints, and to call for even more regulation designed to strengthen consumer rights and remedies. As a *National Journal Opinion Outlook* "Briefing Paper" observes, "Government is seen as the defender of the little guy against powerful and uncontrollable forces. Even those who are generally opposed to regulation will support regulations seen as providing protection against powerful forces that an individual could not otherwise control."[3]

The polls are, or should be, humbling to patronizing regulators and regulatory nihilists alike, since they demonstrate that large majorities are also capable of making subtle and altogether rational distinctions in their attitudes toward regulation. The *National Journal* editors, in an analysis of recent polls, observe that the public continues to demand regulation that restricts business from "bad behavior," while increasingly opposing regulation that hampers competition:

> When the regulation means the government stepping in to protect small companies against ruinous price cutting by larger rivals, or protecting individual consumers against the rapacious price-gouging or shoddy products of corporations, people are all for it.
>
> People who thought there was too much regulation of business commented most frequently that regulation favors big business over small business, protects monopolies, controls or limits competition, interferes with production and free enterprise, allows for price-fixing and creates too much red tape. In other words, *proponents and opponents of regulation shared a common concern—lack of competition.*

The National Journal editors find "little or no evidence to suggest that disaffection with the regulatory activities of government has made more people willing to transfer power to business."[4]

---

3. *National Journal Opinion Outlook Briefing Paper,* vol. 1, no. 19, August 24, 1981 (Washington, D.C.: Government Research Corporation, 1981), p. 2.
4. *National Journal Opinion Outlook Briefing Paper,* vol. 2, no. 5, March 15, 1982 (Washington, D.C.: Government Research Corporation, 1982), pp. 3–5 (emphasis in original).

The public manifests a clear preference for self-help remedies and regulations designed to assure that consumers are provided with sufficient information upon which rationally to base their own decision making. But even stark "command and control" remedies for specified perceived abuses are not rejected. In a 1979 ABC News–Harris poll, 78 percent of a broad citizen sample did not flinch from endorsing a ban on all broadcast advertising of "sugary products" to children, while 72 percent supported a ban on all advertising to children under eight. The *Star* must have missed the audio portion of at least this part of the public's transmission.

Still, the undoubted public dyspepsia evoked by exposure to the term "regulation" must surely be a "sign," as *Time* reads it, confirming the nation's "conservative swing."[5] Yet polls show *no* massive shift in public attitudes toward regulation in general. In the January/February 1979 issue of *Public Opinion*, Seymour Martin Lipset and William Schneider published a comprehensive comparative study of public attitudes toward regulation since the mid-1930s, concluding that

> for over four decades, Americans have been ambivalent in their attitudes toward regulation. A majority has always said they opposed greater regulation, but over the years—as more and more regulation has been enacted—a majority has also voiced approval of existing regulation and indicated that it did not want to roll back the tide.[6]

Whatever has provoked our leaders' acute disaffection with regulation, it was not the sudden or dramatic growth of "antiregulatory sentiment," in the Washington *Star*'s orchestration, "from a squeak to a public howl."[7]

What was it then?

By the late 1970s, consumer entrepreneurial politics were afflicted with acute anemia. What happened between 1965 and 1978, to effect so radical a change?

If the public was not in revolt against regulation, two virulent strains of distemper that darkened the public mood nonetheless provided the animus for a determined business assault on regulation.

5. Stacks, "Rightward On," p. 12.
6. Lipset and Schneider, "The Public View of Regulation," *Public Opinion*, January-February 1979, p. 6.
7. "Kid-Vid Blunder."

First, if we were not a people howling in indignation at regulation, we *were* howling in economic pain and anxiety. And, second, if the public had not abandoned hope for regulation, its faith in the will and capacity of government to fulfill this hope had been profoundly shaken.

Daniel Yankelovich explains that "antigovernment sentiment is really an unhappiness with cost and inefficiency, rather than reflecting a belief that government should not play a major activist role in our society."[8] But he also tells us that

> by the start of the millennial quarter century, the majorities expressing confidence in government had disappeared, and the previously small number of Americans concerned with waste, government indifference, and citizen impotence had grown into large majorities. The changes move in only one direction—from trust to mistrust. They are massive in scale and impressive in their cumulative message. In the course of a single generation Americans have grown disillusioned about the relation of the individual American to his government.[9]

Against this dark backdrop of economic insecurity and political disillusionment, Congress's historic sensitivity to business demands in times of economic stress might in itself have been sufficient explanation for Congress's reaction against business regulation. The extraordinary mobilization of business for political action that took place following the 1974 congressional elections, would have been cause enough. The radical alteration of the incentive structure of Congress, especially the emerging dominance of the media campaign and congressional dependency for career survival upon corporate PACs, would have been explanation enough. The dimming of popular trust in liberal governance, the decimation of liberal leadership in Congress, and the lost conviction of the liberal survivors would have been enough.

The mobilization of business for political action that followed the 1974 congressional elections, in particular, was a truly formidable— and radical—change.

8. *Report to Leadership Participants on 1980 Findings of Corporate Priorities* (New York: Yankelovich, Skelly, and White, 1980), p. 13. The findings in the March 15, 1982, *National Journal Opinion Outlook Briefing Paper* cited above reinforce Yankelovich's conclusions:

> The apparently significant shift against regulation in the past five years might then represent no shift at all in attitudes about what the role of government in the economy *ought* to be—rather, increased opposition to regulation is a result

THE NEW BROTHERHOOD OF BUSINESS SOLIDARITY

In 1969 Edwin Epstein surveyed the domestic economic battlefield and declared the contest between consumer interests and corporate interests a draw.[10] The leveling factor lay not in business's lack of preponderant economic and political resources, but in constraints in the deployment of those resources.

Perhaps the most significant constraint was a simple lack of motivation. Buoyed by economic expansion, prosperity, and confidence, few businessmen felt threatened by the discrete and relatively modest regulatory initiatives of the 1960s. Packaging and labeling standards, uniform interest-rate disclosures, minimum safe-performance standards for automobiles and household goods, while circumscribing narrow areas of corporate autonomy, rarely threatened market shares or penetration. Neither, in an expansive economy in which the costs of meeting such standards could be passed on to consumers, did such regulation greatly threaten profitability. While Ralph Nader may have provoked fear and loathing in Detroit, Nader was not at first perceived as a threat to the greater corporate community. And such political consumer entrepreneurs as Lyndon Johnson, Warren Magnuson, and Philip Hart were themselves perceived as moderates, limited in their regulatory goals, and unthreatening.

Another inhibitor of business's political energy was the political diffidence of most corporate executives. Political activity was not only allocated low corporate priority, it was also not quite respectable. Of course, direct corporate campaign funding was illegal and those legal inhibitions lent an aura of illegitimacy to all forms of political enterprise. Political activism was certainly no path to corporate ascendancy or peer regard. "The best men" were not assigned to Washington offices. Trade associations were starved of funds and confidence. Jeff Joseph, chief lobbyist for the Chamber of Commerce lamented businesses' early lack of spine and spirit: "Business

---

of a shift in perceptions of what the government's role actually has been. The public is more and more aware of the failure of government to carry out its proper regulatory role. Thus the growing opposition to regulation seems to be over issues of management, not issues of authority. [p. 5]

9. Yankelovich, *New Rules: Search for Self-Fulfillment in a World Turned Upside Down* (New York: Random House, 1981), p. 185.

10. Epstein, *The Corporation in American Politics* (Englewood Cliffs, N.J.: Prentice-Hall, 1969), p. 223.

didn't even want to try to fight against something with a consumer handle on it. They weren't that sophisticated, they weren't that well organized. I think a lot of people were concerned about their image."[11]

Such political action on the part of business as took place tended to be narrowly self-serving, preoccupied with sectarian issues directly affecting the individual firm or trade. As Epstein observed in 1969, "Corporations utilize their political resources against each other as frequently as they do against other social interests. Indeed, internecine conflict among business organizations constitutes much of the substance of corporate political activity."[12]

Seeking to settle public fears of excessive corporate political dominance, A. A. Berle, Jr., in 1963 assured Americans that "there is no high factor of unity when several hundred corporations in different lines of endeavor are involved."[13] Even in making campaign contributions, businessmen displayed a lack of ideological aggression. Recently, a Chamber of Commerce political strategist commented contemptuously on business's traditional practice of securing political access by funding opposing candidates in close races. "I keep telling people they might as well give that money to charity."[14]

By 1974, however, regulation and politics had got business's attention. While the late sixties and early seventies had seen passage of many new consumer and environmental, civil rights, and occupational health laws—with their promise of benefits and relief to broad public constituencies—the seventies brought home to business the impact of regulation implemented and enforced: the intended restraints; the costs, burdens, and unintended by-products of regulation; and the trials and errors of new, or newly stimulated, bureaucracies, implementing Congress's imperfectly fashioned works. There were real constraints; real paperwork burdens; real costs. There were the cumulative, sometimes overlapping or inconsistent, burdens of regulatory schemes independently conceived and structured. The Senate Commerce Committee had hardly been alone in its enthusiasm for regulatory enterprise. David Vogel

11. John F. Kennedy School of Government, "Michael Pertschuk and the Federal Trade Commission," Case Program No. 881, discussion draft (1981), p. 17.

12. Epstein, *Corporation in American Politics*, p. 227.

13. Quoted in ibid., p. 229.

14. Richard I. Kirkland, Jr., "Fat Days for the Chamber of Commerce," *Fortune*, September 21, 1981, p. 155.

counts more than 25 separate federal regulatory laws enacted between 1967 and 1973.[15]

Although evidence of business's appreciation is lacking, surely
the Federal Trade Commission can take at least partial credit for
stimulating its political revitalization. Under four Republican chairmen, the commission had redeployed its limited human resources
away from trivial "mail bag cases"—such as those challenging "bait
and switch" advertising—against small and easily intimidated businesses, yielding little tangible or lasting consumer benefit. It had not
only expanded the numbers, quality, and vigor of its human resources, but, in growing, had shifted steadily toward priority economic targets with broad consumer and economic impact, such as
challenges to oligopoly, the abuse of market power by dominant
firms, and conglomerate mergers.

By 1978 the impact of the Magnuson-Moss Act was at last imminent. The fifteen industrywide trade regulation rules (such as those
directed at used car and funeral sales practices) initiated in the mid-
seventies had wound their tortuous course through the rule-making labyrinth.[16] Now, poised upon the threshold of promulgation,
they threatened to upset "business as usual" for tens of thousands
of small, but influential, businessmen and professionals. Even the
commission's non-regulatory ventures, such as its life-insurance
cost disclosure and generic drug substitution studies and model

15. Among these, Vogel lists the most significant as the National Environmental
Policy Act (1969), the Occupational Health and Safety Act (1970), the Consumer
Product Safety Act (1972), and the Clean Air Act Amendments (1970). (Vogel, "Business Finds a Winning Combination on Capitol Hill," *San Jose Mercury News,* December 23, 1979, p. 5B.)

16. While the commission had issued a number of trade regulation rules prior to the
Magnuson-Moss Act, they didn't cause much concern. Whether this was due to the
lack of enforcement teeth, or their frequently trivial subject matter (*e.g.,* the misrep-
resenting of the leather content of men's belts), industry groups never bothered to
challenge them.

But with the commission's new authority under the Magnuson-Moss law to get civil
penalties for rule violations, industry groups began to view with alarm the commission's growing enthusiasm for rule making. In 1975 and 1976, the commission started
no fewer than sixteen separate rule makings, covering a wide range of practices and
industries, many of which had never before been subject to effective federal regulation. While many of the rule proposals were ultimately to be trimmed or dropped as
the rule making proceedings unfolded, many of the initial proposals were ambi-
tious—and, to the industries affected, alarming.

In 1975, industry observers must have viewed themselves as involuntary in-
ductees to the FTC's rule-of-the-month club. In that year alone, the commission
began nine new rules and republished three 1974 rule-making proposals to take

state laws gravely threatened crucial market strategies.[17] The commission was embarked on inquiries that threatened the economic bulwarks of trades and industries: protective, guildlike state regulation; the manipulation of the voluntary standards system by dominant firms and technologies; the dissonance between 600 million dollars in television advertising to motivate to three-, four-, and five-year-olds and ancient common law strictures shielding children from commercial exploitation.[18] The fear and anger generated by these initiatives were compounded by the uncommon competence, determination, and aggressiveness of the FTC staff—too often seen, however unjustly, as zealotry and inquisition. The animosity was also fueled by the sometimes self-righteous independence of the commission from traditional avenues of influence: the Washington Bar, the White House, Congress.

In the mid-seventies, there were gestating within the womb of the FTC alone as many as thirty to forty major investigations, studies, cases, and rule-making proceedings, each as potentially significant—and as threatening to some segments of business—as the truth-in-lending bill or the fair packaging and labeling bill, business *causes célèbres* of a decade earlier.

"You have managed to alienate the leading citizens of every town and city in Kentucky" Senator Wendell Ford wryly observed to me,

---

advantage of the new Magnuson-Moss Act: the Credit Practices Rule (40 *Federal Register* 16347, April 11, 1975); the Vocational Schools Rule (40 *Federal Register* 21048, May 15, 1975); the Food Advertising Rule (40 *Federal Register* 23086, May 28, 1975); the Mobile Home Rule (40 *Federal Register* 28334, May 29, 1975); the Prescription Drug Rule (40 *Federal Register* 24031, June 4, 1975); the Hearing Aid Rule (40 *Federal Register* 26646, June 24, 1975); the Cellular Plastics Rule (40 *Federal Register* 30842, July 23, 1975); the Health Spa Rule (40 *Federal Register* 34615, August 18, 1975); the Funeral Practices Rule (40 *Federal Register* 39901, August 24, 1975); the Protein Supplements Rule (40 *Federal Register* 41144, September 5, 1975); the Over-the-Counter Drug Rule (40 *Federal Register* 52631, November 11, 1975); and an Amendment to the Holder in Due Course Rule (40 *Federal Register* 53506, November 18, 1975).

In 1976, the commission made four new rule-making proposals: the Used Car Rule (41 *Federal Register* 1089, January 6, 1976); the Eyeglasses Rule (41 *Federal Register* 2399, January 16, 1976); amendments to the original 1971 Care Labeling Rule (41 *Federal Register* 3747, January 26, 1976); and the Antacid Rule (41 *Federal Register* 14534, April 6, 1976).

After this initial post-Magnuson-Moss frenzy of rule making, the pace slowed down. Indeed, while I was chairman, the commission made only three new rule proposals: the Home Insulation Rule (42 *Federal Register* 59678, November 18, 1977); the Standards and Certification Rule (43 *Federal Register* 57269, December 7, 1978); and the Children's Advertising proceeding (February, 1978).

17. After several years of investigation, the FTC staff issued a report on life insur-

proceeding to call the roll: "Lawyers, doctors, dentists, optometrists, funeral directors, real estate brokers, life insurance companies and salesmen, new and used car dealers, bankers, loan companies and other credit suppliers, Coca-Cola bottlers. . . ." While we took perhaps perverse pride in the ubiquity of our offenses, as an index of the efficient allocation of regulatory resources, a Chamber of Commerce representative was graciously proferring the consoling embrace of "membership in the FTC victims' alumni association."[19] Perhaps the clearest insight was to come from a public-opinion expert enlisted by the cereal manufacturers in their noble crusade to preserve advertising to five-year-olds. He told me without unneeded embellishment, "You hit the money nerve." And a Washington lawyer of that elegant breed known as "rainmakers" said, "You woke the sleeping giant."

Preserving competition, restraining deceptive advertising, and setting minimum standards of fair dealing are properly viewed as in the long-term interests of a healthy business system—if not the short-term interests of the individual companies charged. The FTC has always played a conservative or conserving role in assuring that the real needs of business are met. Thus even the "Tyrannosaurus rex" of the regulatory agencies—the FTC of the seventies—was still sharply constrained in its consumer initiatives by its instinctive

---

ance cost disclosure in 1979 that recommended a model state disclosure law. The staff report, echoing the conclusions of many students of the industry, found that consumers could not evaluate the cost of competing life insurance policies because there was no standard measure of comparison. As a consequence, some policies offering only a very low rate of return sold better than policies offering substantially better returns. Further, with respect to the savings element of whole life policies, consumers could not compare the rate of return with competing forms of investment. That difficulty caused substantial consumer injury, since the commission's staff had found that the average aggregate rate of return on all outstanding whole life insurance policies was only 1.3 percent! The staff report recommended a model buyer's guide and cost disclosure format to be adopted by the states.

A similar "model state law proposal" made in 1978 grew out of a rule-making proceeding started in 1975. A staff report recommended legislation to permit pharmacists to advertise or disclose prices for prescription drugs. Due partly to the fact that the commission had backed away from its earlier intention to preempt state laws in this area, the report received a more favorable response than the life insurance report, and several states adopted the recommendations in whole or in part.

18. Bailey Morris, "Foes of Child Ad Curbs Devised Strategy Here," *Washington Star*, March 7, 1979.

19. Patrick Riordan and Ed Zuckerman, "Behind FTC Foes in Congress are Foes with Funds," *Philadelphia Inquirer*, December 23, 1979.

deference to the privileged—and essential—role of business in our economy. Even the most drastic remedies contemplated, such as the "infamous" ban on children's advertising,[20] while "pinching the money nerve," would not have been a serious threat to the economic viability of broadcasters or cereal companies. Nevertheless, the commission did prove less diligently deferential to business than Congress would tolerate.

By 1978 the Carter regulators—looming as fearsome and demonic to business as Lloyd Cutler (counsel for the automobile manufacturers)[21] and the Tobacco Institute had earlier been to consumer and public-health advocates—generated great, not always rational, fears of new and accelerating regulatory burdens, the loss of business autonomy, and threats to entrenched market strategies and market power. George Meany's boast that the 1974 elections had produced a "veto-proof Congress" evoked despair among business leaders. With gallows humor, one predicted that the cause of business would be saved by the political might of the environmental movement: "We can get them to put the corporation on the endangered species list."[22]

More and more businessmen concluded, not irrationally, that creeping government encroachment upon their autonomy had to be resisted by direct political action. Some stepped cooly and gingerly into politics; others reacted emotionally, driven by exaggerated fear of government oppression; others indulged their ideological zeal, drawing new confidence from the ascendant Chicago economists' worship of business and markets. Some were simply reacting belatedly to the successful strategies of the public interest entrepreneurs. Whatever the causes, business now elevated politics to a high priority and poured organizational resources into political action.

By 1974 the foundations had been laid for a political mobilization effort by business of a scope and breadth for which only the industrial mobilization of World War II provides a sufficiently heroic, if extreme, analogy.[23] If martial imagery appears unnecessarily hyperbolic, here are the words of Kaiser Aluminum Chairman Cornell

20. "Statement of the United States Chamber of Commerce on Proposed Amendments to the Federal Trade Commission Act to the Consumer Subcommittee of the Senate Commerce Committee," mimeographed, March 19, 1982, p. 24.

21. For more background on Lloyd Cutler, see Mark Green, *The Other Government: The Unseen Power of Washington Lawyers* (New York: Grossman, 1975).

22. Vogel, "Business Finds a Winning Combination," p. 5B.

23. Much of the material in the next few pages is based on the analysis, observations, and data of Thomas Edsall from his series on the strength of business lobbies in Washington published in the *Baltimore Sun*, February 25, 26, and 27, 1980.

Maier: "This is war. The battle is not over our economic system. The battle is over our political system."[24]

Horizontally among firms within industries, jointly among industries, vertically within companies, structures of political coordination and cooperation have proliferated, from the chief executives of the major industrial and financial firms politically united in the Business Roundtable to the 2,700 local congressional action committees of the Chamber of Commerce, which make up a network of close personal friends and supporters of congressmen and other political leaders.

The Business Roundtable, born in 1972, rapidly became both the preeminent lobbying institution and a symbol to all industry of the priority and legitimacy of political action by business. Made up of chief executive officers (CEO's) who, in *Fortune's* worshipful prose, "head the industrial, financial and commercial institutions commanding the heights of the U.S. economy," the uniqueness of the Roundtable lies in its commitment to the participation of CEO's as its active front-line troops, without surrogates, in both policy formation and direct lobbying activities. The Roundtable altered the role model for corporate statesmanship. If Irving Shapiro, Reginald Jones, and Fletcher Byrom could devote their energies to the visible and aggressive pursuit of a political agenda, then so could all. The Roundtable both spawned and reflected the reallocation of business's human and material resources to political action; new alliances and structures for coordination; and the rapid integration of the emerging new information storage, retrieval, and communication technologies in the service of corporate business political advocacy.

The Chamber of Commerce, easily dismissed in the sixties, as a feeble and discredited vestigial organ, took on new sheen and gloss. Though it speaks for the grassroots of American business, the small local entrepreneurs, its new energizing force and leadership were initiated by the barons of corporate politics: Bryce Harlow of Procter & Gamble; William Whyte of U.S. Steel; Albert Borland of General Motors. Between 1974 and 1980, the Chamber of Commerce doubled its membership to 165,000 companies and trebled its annual budget to $68 million.[25] Through aggressive new leadership, it pio-

24. Thomas B. Edsall, "Business Learns to Play New Politics," *Baltimore Sun*, February 25, 1980, p. A7.
25. Thomas B. Edsall, "Business Coalitions Form to Win Congressional Clout," *Baltimore Sun*, February 27, 1980, p. A6; Kirkland, "Fat Days," pp. 144–45.

neered the seeding of political action committees and direct mail and other technologically sophisticated grassroots organizing techniques, many of them shamelessly cribbed from the political arts developed by the public-interest entrepreneurs. In the words of one of its latter-day presidents, the Chamber of Commerce would now be known as "a communications conglomerate."[26] Just as Nader had understood that the path to the sensibilities of Chairman Harley Staggers of the House Commerce Committee ran through the sympathies and access of his physician son-in-law, so the Chamber of Commerce developed its roster of "golden bullets," dear friends and bosom business associates of each congressman.[27]

Another enterprise dedicated to filling the business lobbying gap was the National Federation of Independent Businesses. "Unlike most business organizations which serve a variety of communications and social purposes in addition to lobbying, the NFIB exists entirely to exercise political influence," Thomas Edsall observes. "Its 596,000 members contribute between $35 and $500 based on each firm's willingness to pay, exclusively for political leverage in Washington and some state capitals."[28]

These umbrella organizations in turn coordinate the lobbying efforts of individual corporations, trade associations, public relations firms, and Washington lawyer-lobbyists, all of whom, in turn, have flourished and multiplied.

The Business Roundtable may be said to represent the conglomeration of corporate political action. At least as significant has been the backward integration of political action from the once isolated and not quite respectable Washington representative up to the CEO, down through the corporate hierarchy to mid-level executives and employees, and outward to stockholders, suppliers, and distributors. ARCO, for example, now spends an estimated $1 million annually to support regional political action committees separate from

---

26. Kirkland, "Fat Days," p. 144. The communications arsenal of the Chamber of Commerce includes a biweekly newspaper, *Washington Report;* a monthly magazine, *Nation's Business;* a telephone "hotline" that, it is claimed, can generate 12,000 phone calls to legislators within twenty-four hours; radio programs; and a television show, "It's Your Business," syndicated to 137 television stations (ibid., pp. 144–55 passim). In April 1982 the Chamber inaugurated a nationwide satellite television network, the American Business Network (Biznet), unabashedly calling it "the most effective tool ever devised to influence legislation" ("The Chamber Will Try High-Tech Politicking," *Business Week,* December 7, 1981, p. 46).
27. Edsall, "Business Learns to Play New Politics," p. A7.
28. Edsall, "Business Coalitions Form," p. A6.

list disclosure rule supported by his congressman will remember nothing else as the next election approaches, while citizen consumers, even those who may benefit, remain blissfully unaware of the rule *or* the vote.

But the meticulous recruitment, organizing, and propaganda that characterize the new works of the Chamber of Commerce and other business grassroots organizing lobbies add a less obvious, but perhaps more significant, increment to the political balance: the structuring of the congressman's political environment. The process begins with the overstimulation of the grassroots. The Chamber of Commerce's dispatches from the domestic front in Washington to its members are not fastidious or restrained in their characterization of pending regulatory threats. Indeed, its bulletins display uncommon creativity and a lurid imagination.

I met one day in 1979 with a delegation of fearful small businessmen from Spokane, Washington, who had just come from legislative briefings at U.S. Chamber of Commerce headquarters. They had learned that the FTC was the wickedest of all Washington agencies. But when I asked what it was specifically that we were doing that most troubled them, they hesitated. One of them thought for a moment, then replied, "regulating children's advertising."

"But," I asked, puzzled, "how could that rule affect you at all?"

To my surprise, I learned from their response that the FTC's rule proposals, which would have restricted TV advertising directly to very young children, had been characterized by the Chamber as the first step in a scheme of regulation ultimately designed to bar the local haberdasher from advertising his annual back-to-school sale.

In the spring of 1980, Bill Moyers devoted a segment of his television journal to an examination of the FTC's difficulties with Congress.[34] In the course of our conversations, he told me that he had first been drawn to an examination of the FTC by the laments of a friend, his "Everyman," a Mineola, Long Island, druggist and member of the local Chamber of Commerce, who had complained bitterly that FTC regulations were driving him to the brink of despair. Yet, when Moyers, in the course of preparing his program, sat down with his friend to elicit his specific complaints, the druggist was unable to identify a single FTC case or rule that in any way affected his business.

It does appear that the level of intensity of local businesses' fear

34. PBS, *The Politics of Regulation*, "Bill Moyers' Journal," February 24, 1980.

and loathing of the FTC and other regulatory agencies was a product not simply of informed rational concern, but of irrational fear generated by the Chamber and other trade associations more concerned with stimulating the fervor of business rebellion than with scrupulousness in reporting. But it is not just that the organized grassroots campaigns generated exaggerated fear and hysteria among businessmen. There were the marshaling and deployment of local businessmen, the letters, mailgrams, calls, insistent deputations to Washington, and, during congressional recesses, confrontations at every turn with businessmen stationed and primed, seething with outrage at the dread regulators.

Is it any wonder that congressmen begin to perceive that *everyone*, not just the businessman, is aroused over regulation? They may note polls to the contrary with puzzlement, but polls lack the immediacy of angry petitioners. In a term borrowed from early Hollywood stereophonic hype, the new lobbying has fashioned for the congressman a "sensurround" of anti-regulatory fervor.

And it is this function of the new lobbying that explains why a public still broadly committed to consumer, health, safety, and environmental regulation is perceived even by conscientious and open-minded congressmen as clamoring for relief from all regulation. It is why Senator Danforth can say to me unselfconsciously, "Everywhere I go in Missouri, to every Rotary and Kiwanis luncheon, all I hear are complaints about the FTC." It is why, when Senator Hollings returned from communing with his constituents in South Carolina during the August 1979 recess, he called his staff together and reported that, pressing closely behind inflation, the second most troubling public policy issue to the citizens of South Carolina was the excesses of the Federal Trade Commission.

"It's a good thing they passed the anti-lynch laws before you got appointed," Hollings needled me shortly thereafter. "You're like the cross-eyed javelin thrower; you never hit anything, but you sure keep a lot of folks on the edge of their seats."

THE FREE-ENTERPRISE ECONOMISTS AND BUSINESS:
MADE FOR EACH OTHER

To enhance the legitimacy of its deregulatory thrust, business needed to transcend the apparent pursuit of narrow self-interest. It needed a respectable cloth coat of public interest, tailored by authoritative spokesmen perceived as objective truth seekers. In the resurgent free-enterprise economists, business found its public voice. As Grant Gilmore reminds us in his lectures on the history of American law, "There has always been a symbiotic relationship between the academic establishment, which provides the theories, and the economic establishment, which appreciates being told that the relentless pursuit of private gain is the best way of serving public interest."[35]

Businessmen faced both an analytical and political hurdle in showing a causal nexus between government regulation and the sputtering of the nation's economic system. It has not, for example, occurred spontaneously to the citizens of Japan, Sweden, or Germany that regulation was the prime cause of the economic stress that followed upon the congealing of the OPEC oil cartel. Indeed, industrialists (and perhaps even economists) in these countries look upon consumer-oriented regulation as a quality-control stimulus to the international marketability of their products.

The American public, too, while never very enthusiastic about regulation, is slow to conclude that freeing the *Fortune* 500 is the logical road to economic renewal. And, in fact, as Christopher DeMuth, executive director of President Reagan's Task Force on Regulatory Relief, states:

> Clearly, if the new regulatory controls have been a substantial cause of our flagging measured productivity they have also reduced our competitiveness in international markets. Such evidence as can be reduced to numbers, however, fails to convict the newer regulatory programs of being major culprits in diminishing U.S. competitiveness. . . . It is clear that [the] American experience with costly environmental and workplace controls is not radically different from that of our major competitors. Nor do available statistics suggest that regulation has been a dominant cause of our declining productivity growth.[36]

Of course, the teachings of the economists of the Chicago school served a benign and useful public purpose in drawing the attention of consumer advocates, among others, to the public disservice per-

35. Gilmore, *The Ages of American Law* (New Haven, Conn.: Yale University Press, 1977), p. 66.

36. DeMuth, "Domestic Regulation and International Competitiveness," Paper presented at conference on U.S. productivity, Brown University, February 27–28, 1981.

formed by cartel protection regulation supervised by such agencies as the Civil Aeronautics Board (CAB) and the Interstate Commerce Commission (ICC) in the name of the public interest. By the mid-seventies, the deregulation of trucking and airlines had become an ecumenical legislative objective of consumer advocates and (unregulated) business alike. And, as the free-enterprise economists' anti-regulatory rhetoric began to pervade economic debate, airline and trucking deregulation became the liberals' anti-regulatory hedge, the reformers' ideological free lunch.

Recall that it was Ted Kennedy who led the crusade for airline deregulation, to the unaccustomed acclaim of business moderates and economists, yet with the unflagging support of consumer advocates and liberals. Warmed by the response, Kennedy made transportation deregulation a pillar of his presidential primary campaign.

Just as Nader's attacks on the unresponsive regulatory bureaucracy had the unintended side effect of feeding public disaffection and distrust of government, so the enthusiastic embrace of deregulatory rhetoric by liberals tended to lend legitimacy to the attacks of businessmen and economists like Murray Weidenbaum, who pursued the elimination of health, safety, and consumer regulation with a fervor that surpassed their critiques of economic regulation.[37] The deregulatory yeast, once risen, was hard to contain.

So Congressman Marty Russo could make respectable to liberals and conservatives alike his otherwise unfathomable assault on the FTC's funeral-cost disclosure rule with the following moving rhetoric:

> Overregulation is already enough of a problem in the nation. Productivity is being harmed, inflation is running rampant, either we are going to take a stand against unnecessary federal regulation or we aren't.[38]

It is a little difficult to grasp the concept of productivity in funeral production.

A second contribution of the economists to the political needs of business is the dehumanization of pain, suffering, and economic injury. As I have indicated elsewhere, I consider the assessment of prospective costs and benefits an important and appropriate tool in

37. See Murray L. Weidenbaum, *The Future of Business Regulation* (New York: Amacon, 1979).
38. Russo, Letter to colleagues, September 14, 1979.

the shaping of regulatory policy.[39] But the quantifying of injury denatures the debate. Thus, even in developing techniques for cost-benefit analysis, some scholars, such as those at MIT's Center for Policy Analysis, have refused, as a matter of principle, to reduce human injury and death to dollars. Others prove less fastidious.

Since, as we have seen, consumer entrepreneurial politics depends greatly upon the provoking of public outrage at preventable human misery, the cost-benefit calculus, no matter how sensitive, leeches human misery and outrage from the debate. Not only did the economists supply the theories, but their eminence provided businesses' congressional supporters with a new self-confidence and ideological respectability. In turn, business nurtured and rewarded the flowering of neo-classical economics with unstinting financial support and the generous propagation of the neo-conservative faith through such eager institutions as the American Enterprise Institute and Murray Weidenbaum's Center for the Study of Business at Washington University in St. Louis.

The result was further ideological confusion and enhanced opportunity for business to cloak its pet anti-regulatory goals in fashionable deregulatory rhetoric. The earlier pure outrage at corporate injustice displayed by such liberal voices as the *Washington Post*, gave way to ambivalence fed by the new economic wisdom. Such ambivalence may well reflect an appropriately heightened sense of journalistic humility. But the lack of editorial ardor, the diffidence to economic analysis over moral imperative eased the public pressure on congressmen to resist the special interests.

I do not mean to suggest that any or all of the neo-classical economists are insincere or pandering in the celebration of the unfettered marketplace. (Though I suspect that their own market theories postulate that where a healthy demand from business for ideologically compatible economics exists, market incentives help to stimulate the supply.)

I recall the first set of hearings the Senate Commerce Committee held following the surgeon general's report on smoking and health and the resulting effort by the Federal Trade Commission to require a warning in all cigarette advertising. Thirty-eight distinguished physicians, surgeons, and research scientists, nurtured and coordinated by the Tobacco Institute, sought the opportunity to present their views that no causal relationship between smoking and health

39. For a detailed discussion of this matter, see chapter 5.

had been proved. Hearing the testimony, I was satisfied that at least some of these witnesses *were* genuine agnostics on the subject of the causal relationship between smoking and health. I was also aware that the Tobacco Institute and their law firm, Covington and Burling, had combed the scientific universe to discover these thirty-eight. They were not representative. They were indeed, as one research scientist described them, a remnant of the "Flat Earth Society." But the Tobacco Institute had the resources to gather them in Washington, reproduce their testimony, and widely disseminate their views. The tens of thousands of other physicians and scientists who had no doubt that smoking caused cancer were represented only by the spokesman for the American Cancer Society. Yet the witnesses challenging the causal link outnumbered those supporting it by something like four or five to one. Thus the tobacco industry was able by the marshaling of its resources to amplify disproportionately the voice of perhaps genuine, but nevertheless unrepresentative, dissenters. I suspect that the apparent preeminence of the more extreme laissez-faire economists, to say nothing of supply-siders, is distorted by the same phenomenon.

THE DECLINE OF THE CONSUMER ENTREPRENEURS

As business sallied forth, fueled with PAC money and armed with "golden bullets," Congress, as Cleopatra, was not "prone to argue."

In the mid-sixties, Senator Joseph Clark of Pennsylvania, an evangelical reform liberal, asserted that the salvation of democratic reform lay in freeing the congressional Democratic party from the vise grip of party leadership, discipline, patronage, seniority.[40]

The reforms of the 1960s did just that. Coinciding with the advent of the media campaign, they also transformed each senate and congressional race into an open marketplace in which each candidate had to form his own campaign organization and constituency. As the Democratic party (and beleaguered labor) receded as the prime sources of money, organization, and voter support, the congressional political entrepreneur was inexorably drawn toward business. And business, like the friendly local moneylender, was pleased to fill the void.

40. Clark, *Congress: The Sapless Branch* (New York: Harper & Row, 1964).

Business also became the direct beneficiary of the erosion of the broad liberal consensus and confidence that had characterized both public and elite in the sixties. The informal alliance of entrepreneurial congressmen and senators, their staffs, consumer advocates, and an empathetic press had declined in numbers, power, and conviction. As in the Senate Commerce Committee, consumer leaders were gone or going, through death, aging, and political attrition; and as they departed, so did their entrepreneurial staffs. Their successors adjusted to the altered political environment. The political rewards of consumer activism were problematic; the costs, both real and perceived, were heavy. The dogged liberals who would still resist the pleas of single-interest constituencies and the lures of deregulation were, increasingly, politically vulnerable. The converts (or opportunists) who would embrace the new deregulatory hearings were richly rewarded with contributions and business support.

In a time of generalized antipathy toward government, who would trumpet the sponsorship of new laws or defend new regulations? Ironically, the appointment by President Carter of regulatory activists who vowed to take aggressive initiatives *on their own* undercut the incentives for those congressional consumer advocates who earlier had gained political capital by bludgeoning unresponsive regulators into action.

Negative oversight became the functional substitute for legislative initiative. Congressional staffs, which had proliferated and swelled to help draft and shape consumer and environmental laws, had to accommodate, if they were to find justification for their keep, to the new role of criticizing, challenging, and "reforming" administrative initiatives and existing legislation.

Nixon had cemented the alliance of consumer advocates with congressional liberals and the press, which coalesced in their mutual resistance to his efforts to undermine the new corporate restraints. But, just as Nixon had brought *us* together, the Carter administration stimulated the nascent alliance between business and Congress.

The leadership of the consumer movement became increasingly dispirited and ragged. Many of its strongest and most experienced leaders had been drawn off into regulatory roles by the new administration, where their advocacy was muted by structural and political constraints. The new generation of consumer organization

leaders lacked seasoning, sometimes maturity, and the stature
gained only from years of demonstrated performance. First, from
Congress, later from the agencies, many of the most able consumer
advocates within the government—sometimes frustrated, sometimes ready for a less ascetic life—were drawn off into private law or
consulting practice, accelerating the leaching of talent from the public sector to corporate service.

Public-interest groups were strapped for funding. The freshness
and bloom gone from the public-interest movement, the foundations, such as Ford and others, terminated their "seed money." An
administration peopled with public-interest advocates was an
insufficient "enemy" to generate fervor or money-milking anxiety.
Ironically, while the business opposition to government drew energy from the prominent government role of such perceived enemies as Joan Claybrook, Carol Foreman, and myself, and our real,
exaggerated, or imagined outrages galvanized business emotions,
energies, and resource commitment, consumer advocates lost their
Republican and bureaucratic foils. Attacking Joan Claybrook or
Carol Foreman was painful, not exhilarating, while patient understanding was not the stuff of which movements are sustained.

Finally, labor, the mainstay of institutional support for consumer
initiatives, had become increasingly embattled and distracted by
job-threatening economic stress.

The short, happy life of consumer entrepreneurial politics was in
jeopardy.

3

Stoning the National Nanny:
Congress and the FTC in the Late 1970s

INTRODUCTION

On March 1, 1978, the *Washington Post* delivered its editorial judgment on the FTC's children's advertising proposals, the first major initiative taken at the commission since I had become chairman, less than a year earlier. The *Post* was not pleased.

The FTC as National Nanny

The Federal Trade Commission has now agreed to consider imposing major restrictions on television advertisements aimed at young children. The primary goal of the proposal is to reduce the amount of sugar children eat. Few people, least of all thoughtful parents, will disapprove of that goal. But the means the FCC [*sic*] is considering are something else. It is a preposterous intervention that would turn the agency into a great national nanny.

The proposal has three parts (or "options," as the staff naturally describes them): A complete ban on advertising on programs aimed at children under 8 years of age; a ban on all ads on programs aimed at children under 12 for those sugar-coated products most likely to cause tooth decay; and a requirement that if ads for other heavily sugared products appear on programs aimed at children under 12, such ads be balanced by separate dental and nutritional ads.

Now, it is true that children watch many hours of television and see thousands of advertisements that cause them to demand that their parents buy certain products, mostly candy and cereals with huge amounts of sugar in them. And parents often yield to those demands, with the result that children eat more sugar than is good for them—

69

from which the FTC's staff concluded that government must do something about the ads to protect the children.

But what are the children to be protected from? The candy and sugar-coated cereals that lead to tooth decay? Or the inability or refusal of their parents to say no? The food products will still be there, sitting on the shelves of the local supermarket after all, no matter what happens to the commercials. So the proposal, in reality, is designed to protect children from the weaknesses of their parents—and the parents from the wailing insistence of their children. That, traditionally, is one of the roles of a governess—if you can afford one. It is not a proper role of government.

The source of the "National Nanny" editorial was not *Broadcasting* magazine or a Washington spokesman for the Association of National Advertisers or the American Association of Advertising Agencies, but the "liberal establishment organ." It came, as one of the advertising trade association Washington representatives told me with mingled delight and disbelief, "not from *our* guys but from *your* guy."

Worse, the form it took was ridicule. It would have been damaging enough had the *Post* raised sober questions about the First Amendment implications of the contemplated advertising ban, but to trivialize the children's advertising issue was devastating—a sign to the broadcast, grocery manufacturing, and advertising industries that the Federal Trade Commission's proceeding was fair political game—and to any congressmen tempted legislatively to abort the proceeding, a sign that the political risks would be minimal.

But the editorial helped undermine the commission's political standing in an even more fundamental way: it ceded to the opponents of such rule making the single most powerful political symbol upon which we had depended for our political shield against congressional interference—the defense of the family.

From the beginning, we had sought to frame the issue as an inescapable and conservative extension of the common law's historic strictures against the commercial exploitation of minors. Were there not limits, we asked, well within that legal tradition, upon the calculated effort to transform three-, four-, and five-year-olds in their own homes into programmed pleaders for advertised products? Nor was this concern for the family a mere rhetorical device. In launching its inquiry, the commission was indeed responding to the formal petitions and pleadings of parents, teachers, pediatricians, dentists, and others representing mainstream organizations concerned with family health and welfare.

I must confess—and it is an especially galling confession for a regulator whose credentials (and press notices) have trumpeted his political sensitivity—that before embarking on the children's advertising initiative, I had indeed made a rough political calculation and concluded that it would be relatively immune from political attack. Of course, I understood that the initiative would be enormously threatening to the industries involved, both directly and indirectly. I knew well that there was perhaps no U.S. industry so politically intimidating to Congress as the broadcasters. And I knew that they would find a sympathetic hearing on the Hill. But I judged that most prudent senators and congressmen would long hesitate before enlisting on the perceived side of "junk food" advertisers against the health and well-being of the American child and family.

Though there had been earlier rumblings, signs and portents, especially in Congress, the *Post* editorial served jarring notice that we consumer advocates and regulators were losing our hold on the symbols of the debate, at least in Washington. Now it was the commission—not amoral business—that allegedly threatened to undermine the moral fibre and authority of the family by seeking to substitute government-imposed censorship for parental discipline. Of course, once the issue was framed in these terms, there was no way we could win.

There is an intriguing parallel between this loss of the key symbol of debate and the fate of the automobile industry in the 1960s at the hands of Ralph Nader. There, the industry had for many years successfully characterized automobile safety as an issue of individual responsibility. So long as crash injuries were attributable to the "nut behind the wheel," government intervention to force safety performance standards on cars lacked legitimacy.

But Nader seized the symbol. It was the failure of the manufacturer to safely package passengers within the vehicle to avoid the bloodshed caused by the "second collision"—the contact of the passenger's body with the car's interior—that determined the severity of injury or death, Nader argued. The responsibility, therefore, rested squarely with the manufacturer—a responsibility, congressional investigation determined, that the manufacturers had dismally neglected.

Yet the negligent design of automobiles could not have become a salient issue of public policy so long as auto safety remained an issue primarily perceived as one of individual responsibility—just as children's advertising lacked political saliency when characterized as an issue of parental, rather than advertiser, responsibility.

Charles Lindblom argues that business enjoys grossly disproportionate influence over political decision making not only directly, through its unique political resources, but indirectly, through indoctrination, as the amplified voice in a "rigged, lopsided" marketplace of ideas.[1]

Lindblom also observes that to win, business usually need not convince citizens that the policies it favors are right, but has only to sow sufficient doubt and confusion to dissipate any contrary public consensus and will to act.

In apparent defiance of Lindblom's thesis, consumer entrepreneurial politics flourished in the late sixties and early seventies, despite business opposition, supported by a broad public consensus skillfully nurtured and shepherded by the consumer entrepreneurs.

But by the mid-seventies, the pattern of congressional decision making on consumer issues had begun closely to conform to Lindblom's description: right or wrong, business was mostly getting what it wanted. In the waning days of the seventies, the Carter administration was besieged by an aroused business community poised to pounce upon offending regulators. Those liberal congressmen who survived were in increasing numbers intimidated or indentured to business, and stood aside or joined the revolt against regulation.

One modest task remained for business: to clothe the regulatory revolt in the trappings of reform—for even a willing Congress would not dare go against the consensus that government must serve public purposes, not private ones.

Business and its free-market economist auxiliaries had pumped Washington full of the rhetoric of deregulation and regulatory reform.

Initially, they had concentrated on economic regulations, universally condemned for unjustified restraints on competition. It was to prove an easy step to spread the mantle of justified regulatory reform from such worthy targets as the ICC and the CAB to the spu-

1. Lindblom, *Politics and Markets* (New York: Basic Books, 1977), p. 212.

rious reform of regulations whose essential vice was that they threatened to disturb profits or market power.

The noisome passage of the Federal Trade Commission Improvements Act of 1980[2] perhaps illustrates as vividly as any congressional chronicle the triumph of business in diverting public attention and congressional outrage from consumer injury to business's hardships at the hands of the regulators.

This chronicle is not intended to serve as a case study in injured regulatory innocence. In Chapter 2 I acknowledge our sometime sins of regulatory overreaching. And, in keeping with longstanding FTC tradition, I have always been especially forthcoming in acknowledging the errors of my predecessors.

Congress did not act simply to curb instances of regulatory overreaching or to assure that such errors would not recur. Such valid regulatory reform would scarcely have been evidence of undue business political influence.

At one time or another during the commission's legislative travail, at least one congressional committee or house voted overwhelmingly to abort virtually every major FTC rule making, case, or investigation that had aroused the concern of affected industries or even individual companies. Some of these congressional foreclosures actually became law. Others succeeded when, menaced by the imminent threat of congressional action, the commission itself backed down.

A procession of diverse business coalitions—united by what the Chamber of Commerce spokesman proclaimed as membership in the society of "victims of the FTC"[3]—engulfed Congress, beseeching it to debar threatened FTC rule making: the childrens' advertising rule-making proceeding; our funeral-cost disclosure rule; our disclosure rule covering used car defects and warranties; our model state insurance cost disclosure law; our proposed rule to inhibit discrimination against small, innovative competitors and consumers through abuse of the voluntary standards system; even the venerable commission ruling, tediously sustained in the courts, requiring the chronically overreaching sellers of *Encyclopaedia Britan-*

2. Federal Trade Commission Improvements Act of 1980, Pub. L. No. 96–252, 94 Stat. 375.

3. Patrick Riordan and Ed Zuckerman, "Behind FTC Foes in Congress are Foes with Funds," *Philadelphia Inquirer*, December 23, 1979.

nica to present a three-by-five-inch card at the door identifying themselves, contrary to practice, as *sales* representatives.

Nor did analytic nicety inhibit the lobbyists from equally impassioned pleas against FTC efforts to strike down excessive government and private regulation. So, in the name of regulatory reform, Congress was asked to block the FTC's anti-monopoly case against the Sunkist agricultural cooperative and *all* of our studies, rules, and cases challenging overregulation of the professions.[4]

With scattered exceptions, the deregulatory posse shunned debate on the substance of these rules and cases. Instead, on behalf of oppressed business everywhere, they drew for Congress a collective portrait of the FTC as:

1. Unelected bureaucrats defying the will of Congress (and hence the people);

2. Straightjacketers of competition, foulers of the nest of innovation and productivity (and hence contributors to the Japanese competitive menace);

3. Defilers of the sanctity of state regulatory prerogatives and the time-honored traditions of ethical self-regulation, especially among the learned professions;

4. Tramplers on the due process rights of corporate citizens;

5. National nannies and beastly burdeners of business.

We certainly stimulated the creativity of congressional phrase makers. Among the commission's congressional picadors was Con-

---

4. In the Sunkist case, the commission charged Sunkist with monopolizing the Western citrus fruit industry by, among other things, using exclusive dealing contracts with commercial packers. Under those contracts, packers were prohibited by Sunkist from handling citrus fruit from non-member growers and from dealing with competitors. Sunkist allegedly controlled 75 percent of the total production of certain citrus fruits in the West. Congress saw the suit as an attack on the limited antitrust exemption given to agricultural cooperatives, which was originally intended to protect small family farmers. But Sunkist, a co-op in form, was no small farmer: its annual sales were more than $500 million, making it a giant in the industry.

One of the few commission programs to win the praises of Milton Friedman and Edward Kennedy alike is the commission's "occupational deregulation" program, designed to challenge certain state and private restrictions on the delivery of professional services. In the consumer protection area, the commission's Eyeglasses Rule struck down state laws that prohibited truthful advertising by eyewear sellers, based in part on studies indicating that prices were substantially lower in jurisdictions that permitted price advertising. In the antitrust area, the commission challenged such

gressman William Frenzel, whose rhetoric scaled the heights of outrage:

> [T]he FTC is such a mess that one hardly knows where to begin discussing its problems. It epitomizes all the things that Americans find excessive, unnecessary, wasteful, duplicative, and repugnant about regulatory agencies.
>
> But the FTC is more than just your ordinary pain-in-the-neck. It is a king-sized cancer on our economy. It has undoubtedly added more unnecessary costs on American consumers who it is charged with protecting, than any other half dozen agencies combined.
>
> It is bad enough to be counterproductive and therefore highly inflationary, but the FTC compounds its sins by generally ignoring the intent of the laws, and in writing its own whenever the whimsey strikes it. It indicts by press release. Due process is a phrase foreign to it. It invents its own extra-legal criteria for harassment. It engages in witch-hunts, demanding information which costs consumers dearly, for cases it never intends to complete.
>
> Ignoring Congress can be a virtue, but the FTC's excessive nosethumbing at the legislative branch has become legend. In short, the FTC has made itself into a virulent political and economic pestilence, insulated from the people and their representatives, and accountable to no influence except its own caprice.[5]

Simply put, the FTC was "a rogue agency gone insane."

Fortunately, I need not rely upon my own wounded innocence to support the claim that these charges were largely nonsense. Several observers whose objectivity is far less suspect than my own have since exposed as dross the articulated congressional complaints against the FTC.[6] And I, for one, have found their accounts fascinating and wholly persuasive.

---

conduct as a doctors' agreement to boycott Medicaid patients in order to coerce a Michigan Medicaid agency to increase fees paid to doctors; illegal threats by a small town's only doctors to boycott the local hospital's emergency-room patients if the hospital persisted in plans to recruit a new physician competitor to practice at the hospital; and conspiracies in Pennsylvania, Washington, and other states to boycott physicians who work on a salary for innovative, low-cost health maintenance organizations, by excluding these doctors from hospitals, participation in Blue Shield, local medical associations, and malpractice insurance coverage.

5. U.S., Congress, House, *Congressional Record*, 96th Cong., 1st sess., November 14, 1979, 125, no. 161: 10,757–58.

6. Susan Tolchin and Martin Tolchin, *Dismantling America* (Boston: Houghton Mifflin Co., forthcoming); Robert A. Katzmann, *Regulatory Bureaucracy: The Federal Trade Commission and Antitrust Policy* (Cambridge, Mass.: M.I.T. Press, 1981), pp. 145–59, 214–15; William E. Kovacic, "The Federal Trade Commission and Congressional Oversight of Antitrust Enforcement, 1969–1980," *Tulsa Law Journal*, in press.

But I offer, for your enlightenment, a modest sampling of misdirected congressional indignation at the National Nanny in her nefarious guises:

Unelected Bureaucrats Defying the Will of Congress

As William Kovacic has generously documented, the outrage of Frenzel and others follows hard upon a decade of congressional flagellation of the FTC for its lack of aggressiveness.

Thus, in 1971, Senate appropriations subcommittee chairman Gale McGee lectured the new FTC chairman, Miles Kirkpatrick:

> The Commission's duty is to strike blows in behalf of the consumer. . . . Too often it has been either shy or bashful—gun-shy. . . . I think the mistakes you are to make ought to be mistakes in doing and trying rather than playing safe in not doing.[7]

The next year, McGee returned to his theme:

> Stay with it and flex your muscles, clench your fists, sharpen your claws, and go to it.
> We think this is desperately important in the interest of the Congress, whose creature you are, and the consumer whose faith and substantive capabilities in surviving hang very heavily upon what you succeed in doing.[8]

In 1971 another new Nixon FTC chairman, Lewis Engman, appeared before the Senate Commerce Committee for confirmation. Consumer subcommittee chairman Frank Moss charged him:

> Mr. Engman, there is no post in government more crucial to the interest of consumers and business alike than chairmanship of the FTC. The commission's broad mandate to police the nation's marketplace of unfair and deceptive practices is broad and powerful.
> Yet, for much of its recent life, the commission has rightly been derided as puny, ineffectual, and irrelevant to the real needs of consumers and competition.

7. U.S., Congress, Senate Committee on Appropriations, *Agriculture, Environmental and Consumer Protection Appropriations for Fiscal Year 1972, Hearing before a Subcommittee of the Senate Committee on Appropriations*, 92d Cong., 1st sess., 1971, p. 2673.

8. U.S., Congress, Senate, Committee on Appropriations, *Agriculture, Environmental and Consumer Protection Appropriations for Fiscal Year 1973, Hearings before a Subcommittee of the Senate Committee on Appropriations*, 92d Cong., 2d sess., 1972, p. 1483.

Under your two predecessors, Weinberger and Kirkpatrick, the commission has taken on new life beginning with the search for strong and imaginative, rigorous developers and enforcers of the law and reaching out with innovative programs to restore competition and to make consumer sovereignty more than chamber of commerce rhetoric.

Under their direction, the commission has not shied away from tangling with giants of American commerce. That is as it should be.

The commission has stretched its powers to provide a credible countervailing public force to the enormous economic and political power of huge corporate conglomerates which today dominate American enterprise. That is as it should be.

The commission has sought and vigorously pursued legislative authority to make its writ run firmly to reach and irradicate [sic] market abuses. That is as it should be.

This committee has stood in solid support of the commission's efforts. We have not been reluctant to credit a Republican administration with responsibility for introducing new vigor to the "little old lady on Pennsylvania Avenue." We consider it one of our solemn duties to protect the commission from economic and political forces which would deflect it from its regulatory zeal."[9]

Even ranking Republican senator Norris Cotton, fond of referring to himself as a "mossback conservative" complained that the FTC "has had a need for some kind of injunction to pep it up so it would fulfill its mission."[10]

Senator Ted Stevens, now Senate Republican majority whip, piled it on:

I am really hopeful that . . . you will become a real zealot in terms of consumer affairs and some of these big business people will complain to us that you are going too far.

That would be the day, as far as I am concerned.[11]

The children's advertising proceeding evoked a splendid sampling of congressional outrage, some of which, especially First Amendment concern, was genuine (though the posturing of Kellogg's as staunch defender of the free speech of five-year-old's was not entirely convincing).

But the charge principally launched by the then ranking Republi-

9. U.S., Congress, Senate, Committee on Commerce, *Nomination of Lewis A. Engman, to Be a Federal Trade Commissioner, Hearings before the Senate Commerce Committee*, 93d Cong., 1st sess., 1973, pp. 4–5.

10. Ibid., p. 25.

11. Ibid., p. 31.

can member of the House appropriations subcommittee, Mark Andrews of North Dakota, to support his amendment terminating the proceeding does not admit so tender a judgment.

Andrews erupted with indignation at the effrontery of the commission in illicitly poaching upon the regulatory territory of the Food and Drug Administration:

> The intrusion upon the primary jurisdiction of the FDA is clear. . . . The FDA has the authority, and indeed the responsibility to act on matters of the safety of food as they have the expertise. . . . This is an example of the FTC's intrusive and expansionist nature. . . . The FTC must not be allowed to get away with invading the FDA's jurisdiction.[12]

The House Appropriations Committee found Congressman Andrews's legislative scholarship impeccable and the committee adopted his amendment, which would have barred the commission from regulating the advertising of any food product not banned for human consumption by the FDA.[13]

In his peroration to the House, however, Congressman Andrews overlooked the basic Federal Trade Commission Act, and, more specifically, the Wheeler-Lea Act amendments of 1938, which expressly direct the FTC, *not* the FDA, to police food advertising.

In particular, the FTC is authorized to halt any food advertisement that "fails to reveal . . . consequences which may result from the use of the (food) . . . under such conditions as are customary or usual."[14]

Surely, if sugared cereals or candy rot teeth or contribute to malnutrition, these are "consequences" that fall within the FTC's charge?

One might have forgiven Congressman Andrews's lack of scholarship were it not accompanied by a lapse of legislative memory, since in 1974 his own subcommittee had unanimously *directed* the commission to "achieve . . . effective regulation of children's advertising," noting, pointedly, that "the committee views this as a high priority topic." Indeed, in a rare demonstration of congressional

12. U.S., Congress, House, *Congressional Record,* 96th Cong., 2d sess., September 28, 1978, 124, no. 154: 11,022–24.

13. U.S., Congress, House, Committee on Appropriations, *Departments of State, Justice, and Commerce, the Judiciary and Related Agencies Appropriations Bill, Fiscal Year 1979,* 95th Cong., 2d sess., 1978, H. Rept. 1253, p. 46.

14. Federal Trade Commission Act, 15 *U.S. Code* §§52, 55 (1976).

solicitude, Mr. Andrews's committee urged that "if additional funds are required [for children's advertising regulation] appropriate action should be taken to obtain them."[15] Kovacic demonstrates that the commission's initiative on children's advertising was directly responsive to persistent congressional prodding dating back to 1974.

As late as 1977, after my first hearing before the Senate Appropriations Committee shortly after taking office, the committee encouraged my expressed intention of making children's advertising one of the FTC's highest priorities:

> The [Senate Appropriations] Committee shares the commission's growing concern about the effects of advertising on children. The committee therefore encourages the commission to review its current expenditures to determine if sufficient funds can be made available from fiscal year 1977 resources to implement a viable program in this critical area.[16]

The FTC's alleged defiance of congressional will was also invoked—also as an afterthought—to justify halting the commission's modest effort to call public attention to the life insurance industry's marketing genius in obscuring the incredibly poor investment value of most whole life insurance policies.

On July 10, 1979, I testified before the Senate Commerce Committee on the results of a life insurance cost disclosure study that had been underway at the commission since 1972.[17] I reported that the commission's bureau of economics, in consultation with several leading actuaries, had calculated that the average rate of return on the investment portion of all whole life insurance policies in the hands of consumers in 1977 was 1.3 percent per annum. The commission had concluded—as many other students of life insurance marketing had also concluded—that this low level of return was directly caused by a marketing system that made it virtually impossible for a prospective policy holder—other than an actuary—to compare the interest yields of competing policies and of competing

15. U.S., Congress, House, Committee on Appropriations, *Agriculture, Environmental and Consumer Protection Bill, 1975*, 93d Cong., 2d sess., 1974, H. Rept. 93–1120, p. 88.

16. U.S., Congress, Senate, Committee on Appropriations, *Departments of State, Justice and Commerce, the Judiciary and Related Agencies Appropriation Bill, 1978*, 95th Cong., 1st sess., 1977, S. Rept. 95–285, p. 53.

17. U.S., Congress, Senate, Committee on Commerce, *Hearings on the FTC's Study of Life Insurance Cost Disclosure*, 96th Cong., 1st sess., 1979, p. 2.

investment opportunities. The commission had therefore developed a new *model* state life insurance cost disclosure law for consideration by state insurance commissioners. We did *not* propose federal intervention in insurance regulation.

That hearing was to be my last congenial appearance before the Senate Commerce Committee during my tenure as chairman. The committee members present expressed genuine interest and concern at the commission's findings. Indeed, at the close of the hearings, Chairman Cannon took me aside and indicated, sotto voce, that he had found the report so persuasive that he was reviewing all of his personal policies to determine whether they should be replaced.

The FTC study had been undertaken at the direct behest of the Senate antitrust and monopoly subcommittee following its investigation during the early 1970s into life insurance marketing practices.[18] As recently as 1978, the House commerce oversight and investigations subcommittee had urged the commission to complete its study, calling it "highly desirable," "clearly justified," and "wholly lawful, proper, and appropriate."[19]

None of which forestalled a virulent outbreak of congressional indignation following the life insurance industry's attack of dyspepsia at the report's conclusions.

No murmur of discontent had been heard from the Senate Commerce Committee until the life insurance industry erupted in wrath. *Then* the members discovered the commission's perfidy: "The FTC's insurance investigation is a classic case of an agency running out from under Congress' control," Senator Danforth discovered. "We have to make absolutely certain the FTC will not investigate the insurance industry. If this doesn't work, I don't know what will . . . maybe criminal sanctions."[20]

Chairman Cannon managed to contain his earlier enthusiasm for the FTC report: "What we intend to do . . . is to be sure the FTC keeps its nose out of the investigation of the insurance industry.[21]

18. U.S., Congress, Senate, Committee on Judiciary, *The Life Insurance Industry, Hearings before the Subcommittee on Antitrust and Monopoly,* 93d Cong., 1st and 2d sessions., 1973–74.

19. U.S., Congress, House, Committee on Interstate and Foreign Commerce, *Life Insurance Marketing and Cost Disclosure,* Comm. Print 95–72, 95th Cong., 2d sess., 1978, p. 62.

20. *St. Louis Post-Dispatch,* June 8, 1981; *Washington Post,* November 21, 1979.

21. U.S., Congress, Senate, *Congressional Record,* 96th Cong., 2d sess., February 7, 1980, 126, no. 18: 1211.

On November 20, 1979, the Senate Commerce Committee, by a vote of fifteen to none, adopted an amendment to the FTC Act barring the commission from ever studying insurance—a legislative prefrontal lobotomy. The committee was so intent upon punishing the FTC for its imagined defiance of congressional will that it never considered the only relevant question that was before it as it considered amendments to the commission's basic authority: was it not *now* in the public interest for the commission to examine market and regulatory failures in the insurance industry?

StraightJacketers of Competition, Foulers of the Nest of Innovation and Productivity

On November 14, 1979, in response to the pleas of Congressman Marty Russo of Chicago, the House of Representatives voted 223 to 147 to veto the FTC's proposed funeral-cost disclosure rule. Congressman Bethune's comments fairly represent the tenor of the debate:

> I support the Russo amendment . . . which will forbid the FTC from implementing its proposed "funeral trade regulation rule."
> I do this because I believe Federal regulations have gone too far. Must this country be like Sweden, where it is against the law to spank your child, before we say "no" to the bureaucracy?
> Industry is dying in America because of Federal regulations. It distresses me greatly to see a giant like Chrysler Corp. faltering to its haunches. . . .
> The handwriting is on the wall for the FTC and all Federal bodies to stop killing the American businessman and our economy.[22]

As I have indicated elsewhere, I do not take lightly the general concerns expressed by Congressmen Russo and Bethune. But the FTC's funeral rule, as it had been narrowed and limited by the full commission nine months before Russo offered his amendment, contained nothing more burdensome than these elementary requirements: (1) no more lying by funeral directors about alleged costly legal requirements; (2) a requirement that funeral directors answer reasonable requests for information about the price of funerals over the phone; (3) a prohibition against any funeral director requiring unnecessary and expensive caskets for cremations; and (4)

22. U.S., Congress, House, *Congressional Record*, 96th Cong., 1st sess., November 14, 1979, 125, no. 161: 10,759.

a requirement that each funeral home make available an itemized price list.

Russo's outrage at the impact of this rule upon *productivity* is particularly curious. To the best of my knowledge, undertaking in the United States has not been celebrated for economies of scale. It is, indeed, part of the service sector that, in general, reflects the lowest productivity growth rates within the U.S. economy. There are today some 400 to 500 funeral homes in the Chicago area (Mr. Russo's hometown) and approximately 700 funerals a week.[23] This averages out to less than two funerals per funeral home per week, perhaps not the most enviable record of productivity to defend.

What is manifest from these figures, however, is that in order for each of these funeral parlors to survive, every funeral must produce maximum revenue. Perhaps this is the productivity for which the congressmen sought succor, for it is possible that in Chicago (as in Florida after that state's aggressive elderly citizenry successfully fought for the adoption of a law similar to the commission's proposed rule) the average price of funerals will decline significantly.

"A federal law covering the funeral industry will no doubt lessen competition," protests Mr. Russo. It is true that the FTC rule, like the Florida law, might have decreased the profitability of funerals. But it is hard to comprehend how enhanced opportunity to compare prices could do anything but strengthen competition.

Defilers of the Sanctity of State Regulatory Prerogatives and the Time-Honored Traditions of Ethical Self-Regulation

Ironically, one arena of commission activity that has drawn the enthusiastic support of the American Enterprise Institute and neoclassical economists generally has been the commission's effort to challenge excessive economic regulation of trades and professions. Much of this regulation is, of course, self-imposed through "ethical codes," but in many cases the professions, especially the learned professions, have succeeded in sheltering their guild-like privileges under the umbrella of state regulatory authority, without in any way giving up control.

The FTC challenged the American Medical Association's prohibitions against price advertising by members, attacking these provisions as direct violations of the Sherman Act's strictures against

23. Sam Smith, "FTC's Probe of Funeral Industry Dying on the Vine," *Chicago Tribune*, March 8, 1981, Sect. 1, p. 8.

price fixing among competitors, and was upheld by the U.S. Court of Appeals.

Though no form of economic activity could be a more traditional violation of antitrust principles than price fixing, Newton Minnow, an attorney for the American Medical Association, wrapped his cause in the fashionable rhetoric of the "new federalism." "We are witnessing an unprecedented effort by a federal agency to redefine the fundamental relationships of our system of government. . . . The AMA asks Congress to halt this unintended federal intrusion into decisions which are the legitimate prerogative of the states."[24]

The court considered the states' rights issue and summarily rejected the AMA's argument. Yet an amendment offered on the Senate floor by Senators McClure and Melcher that would in effect have given new immunity from FTC antitrust scrutiny to any conspirator with a graduate degree came within two votes of passage.[25]

Tramplers on the Due Process Rights of Corporate Citizens

As James Q. Wilson observes, "perceptions of the fairness and unfairness of a policy profoundly affect the extent to which it is regarded as legitimate." Denials of due process are indeed a legitimate source of congressional outrage. But pleas of denial of due process may also serve as a convenient device for diverting attention away from the substance and merit of proposed regulation. So it was that the parties to the FTC's children's advertising and voluntary standards proceedings both complained that the commission's rule-making procedures grievously violated their rights to due process.

The authoritative Administrative Conference of the United States had earlier found that the commission was needlessly burdening its rule-making process with excess formality, including unrestrained cross-examination.[26] We therefore adopted for the children's proceeding a two-stage hearing process designed to winnow policy and legal argument from factual issues and to provide appropriate restraints on the unlimited examination and cross-examination of wit-

---

24. *Atlanta Constitution*, September 19, 1979.
25. U.S., Congress, Senate, *Congressional Record*, 96th Cong., 2d sess., February 6, 1980, 126, no. 17: 1102–3, 1116. The amendment was defeated by forty-seven votes to forty-five.
26. See Administrative Conference of the United States, "A Report to the Administrative Conference of the United States by the Special Project for the Study of Rule-making Procedures under the Magnuson-Moss Warranty–Federal Trade Commission Act," mimeographed, 1979.

nesses. The food manufacturers and broadcasters maintained that it was a gross violation of their due process rights to apply such procedures to the children's proceeding. The parties to the standards proceeding, on the other hand, insisted that the commission's *failure* to apply the two-stage hearing process in that case was equally an unconscionable denial of *their* due process rights. Congress was sympathetic to both.

National Nannies and Burdeners of Business

Those who plead for relief from the unconscionable burdens of regulation strike a sympathetic chord in the bosoms even of those Americans otherwise chary of business virtue. Latter-day congressmen especially tend to accept business cost and burden estimates, no matter how fantastic, with touching faith.

I myself had spent so much time listening to the fearsome rhetorical blasts of FTC critics like Congressman Frenzel that I was startled and delighted to learn from a most searching Business Roundtable inquiry that the sum of FTC-imposed burdens on Roundtable members was negligible (less than one percent of the cost of federal regulation).[27]

Still, ever alert to new dangers, Congressman Marty Russo warned his fellow congressmen in a "dear colleague" letter (dated September 14, 1979) that "[f]uneral representatives have submitted a study to the Council on Wage and Price Stability which claims that the rule could cost consumers $50,000,000 a year."

Surely one must view with alarm so alarming a study—bearing at least the quiescent imprimatur of the Council on Wage and Price Stability. Upon examination, it appeared that while a copy of the industry study had indeed been *sent* to COWPS, no one there had asked for it, reviewed it, or indeed even recalled seeing it.

Still the funeral industry was entitled to respect for its creativity in inflating its cost estimates by distorting the potential impact of provisions in the commission's initial proposed rule, which *might* have imposed such burdens as requiring funeral directors to maintain a variety of low-cost caskets in their inventory.

But whether or not the fifty million dollar estimate was accurate had become a matter of only academic curiosity by the time of Con-

27. *Cost of Government Regulations Study for the Business Roundtable* (Washington, D.C.: Arthur Andersen and Co., 1979).

gressman Russo's letter, since the commission had already dropped virtually all of the potentially expensive requirements of the proposed rule.

Nevertheless Congressman Russo, displaying the very innovation he justly celebrates, appears simply to have assigned arbitrary costs to the remaining provisions until they again totalled fifty million dollars. It was, after all, a good round figure.

Another unconscionable burden inflicted upon an innocent American enterprise by the FTC was to strain the tolerance of the United States Senate. The commission had subpoenaed from the major cigarette companies all their research data and strategic marketing plans, especially material relating to submerged appeals to teenagers. After the customary dilatory resistance by the industry, which consumed some two years of fierce litigation, the courts routinely upheld the commission's authority to obtain the data. Representatives of all but one of the cigarette companies sat down with the commission staff and negotiated (as is the custom) limiting their submissions to the precise documents that would satisfy the commission's interest. Phillip Morris and the others were thus able to content the FTC staff with submissions that occupied a couple of file drawers.

Brown & Williamson, however, marched to a different drummer. In an act of uncommon corporate citizenship and forthcoming spirit, B&W, which had originally fought the subpoena as oppressively broad, now construed it as broadly as possible, thereupon compiling for the commission fourteen thousand pounds of documents.

Indeed, so proud was Brown & Williamson of its forthcomingness, that its public relations staff alerted all Washington media to the pending delivery of an entire truckload of documents to the FTC. When the truck driver arrived at the commission's loading dock a day too early, with no one but a security guard to witness his mission, breathless Brown & Williamson officials stopped him before he could unload and redispatched him, as scheduled, the next day to unload before the cameras.

A scant few weeks later, the general counsel of Brown & Williamson, displaying photographs of weary employees tediously plowing through great mounds of files, denounced the subpoenas as yet another example of the FTC's "reckless bullying of business."[28]

28. U.S., Congress, Senate, Committee on Commerce, *Oversight of the Federal Trade Commission*, 96th Cong., 1st sess., 1979, p. 93.

Consumer subcommittee chairman Wendell Ford of Kentucky,
home of B&W, was suitably outraged and suitably sympathetic to
Brown & Williamson's plea for limiting the commission's subpoena
authority. Their testimony compelled him to author an amendment
limiting the FTC's investigational authority. "You know there's an
old adage about curiosity killing the cat," he said, "curiosity here
might kill an agency."[29]

There remains only a curious footnote to this tale of commission
abuse of an innocent firm. Squirreled away in Brown & Williamson's
seven tons of corporate files (extracted only after tedious dedication
by the commission's staff) were some rare and exquisite clues to
B&W's marketing morality. It appeared that a marketing strategist's
blueprint for attracting "starters" had led the way to exploiting the
young smoker's vulnerability:

> For the young smoker, the cigarette is not yet an integral part of life, of
> day-to-day life, in spite of the fact that they try to project the image of
> a regular, run-of-the-mill smoker. For them, a cigarette, and the
> whole smoking process, is part of the illicit pleasure category. . . . In
> the young smoker's mind a cigarette falls into the same category with
> wine, beer, shaving, wearing a bra (or purposely not wearing one),
> declaration of independence and striving for self-identity. For the
> young starter, a cigarette is associated with introduction to sex, life,
> with courtship, with smoking "pot" and keeping late studying
> hours.[30]

He advised:

> —Present the cigarette as one of the few initiations into the adult
> world.
> —Present the cigarette as part of the illicit pleasure category of prod-
> ucts and activities.
> —In your ads create a situation taken from the day-to-day life of the

29. Ibid., p. 95.
30. Information about these confidential documents was requested and obtained
by the Congress. Subsequently it was made part of the public record of House
hearings looking into the Reagan administration's cancellation of a federal teenage
anti-smoking campaign featuring actress Brooke Shields. See U.S., Congress,
House, Committee on Energy and Commerce, *Cigarette Advertising and the HHS
Antismoking Campaign, Hearings before a Subcommittee of the House Committee on Energy
and Oversight*, 97th Cong., 1st sess., 1981, p. 66. References herein to these documents are taken solely from the House report and not from the documents themselves, which are being kept under protective order by the commission.

young smoker but in an elegant manner have this situation touch
on the basic symbols of the growing-up, maturity process.
—To the best of your ability, (considering some legal constraints),
relate the cigarette to "pot," wine, beer, sex, etc.
—*Don't* communicate health or health-related points.[31]

B&W adopted many of the ideas contained in this report in the
development of a Viceroy advertising campaign. Thus, in a docu-
ment entitled "Viceroy Strategy," B&W's marketing staff notes re-
peatedly that its advertising campaign must provide consumers
with a rationalization for smoking and a "means of *repressing* their
health concerns about smoking a full flavor Viceroy."[32]

These samples of congressional disingenuousness are, admit-
tedly, choice; they are not atypical.

Yet, typical or not, they certainly manifest business's triumph in
seizing back the symbols of debate from the consumer advocates,
undermining the legitimacy of much regulation, at least in the
minds of Congress, and disarming the preexisting public consensus
supporting consumer regulation.

A procession of companies and industry trade associations under
investigation by the commission were invited to vent their grievances against the FTC during seven days of "oversight" hearings in
the fall of 1979, scheduled by the reconstituted leadership of the
Senate Commerce Committee under its chairman, Howard Cannon, and the consumer subcommittee chairman, Wendell Ford.[33]

Though an occasional token consumer representative was allowed to cite business abuses and consumer injury in support of
commission proceedings or even to criticize the commission for
excessive diffidence with respect to business concerns, the Senate
members husbanded their indignation for FTC transgressions as
viewed through business lenses. At the close of the hearings, the
management of the commission was given an opportunity to respond to the testimony. While defending the commission against
what we considered to be spurious charges, we did not shrink from
confessing error. There were, to be sure, other business criticisms

31. Ibid., p. 67 (emphasis in original).
32. Ibid., p. 67 (emphasis in original).
33. U.S., Congress, Senate, Committee on Commerce, *Oversight of the Federal Trade
Commission*, 96th Cong., 1st sess., 1979.

than those I have selected. In 1974 the Magnuson-Moss Act had, for the first time, authorized the FTC to address consumer injury through broad industrywide rules.[34] Much of the criticism was fairly directed at the overbroadness and potential burdensomeness of rules first *proposed* by the commission in the blush of enthusiasm for rule making following the act's passage.

But we *had* learned. In response to congressional (and other) concerns, we had taken both formal and informal steps to curb unduly threatening, premature rule proposals. In addition, we had embraced regulatory reform amendments before the committee, which had been proposed earlier by the administration on a government-wide basis, designed to assure earlier and greater business participation in the formulation of proposed rules and to strengthen the due process guarantees in the rule-making process. We reaffirmed that endorsement.

But we also recalled for the committee's benefit that not a single criticism throughout the days of industry testimony had been leveled at any final action taken or rule promulgated and implemented by the commission. No witness had testified that the commission had ignored valid industry objections in formulating any final rule.

Even those ills that were arguably genuine, had, therefore, either been cured or were in the process of being cured.

As I was preparing my own testimony to be presented at the close of the Senate oversight hearings, seeking to be responsive, but to defend the commission against charges that were, at best, crudely distorted, I chanced to talk with Ralph Nader on the telephone. I unburdened myself to him about my own frustration at the dignity accorded by the committee to such attacks. One industry witness after another had woven in the minds of senators, otherwise ignorant of the evolution or justification of commission proceedings, a tapestry of FTC arrogance and disdain for due process and reasoned discourse that could only prejudice even the most dispassionate member. I wanted desperately to express my own sense of outrage and anger at the distortions of the commission's record, and I told Ralph that I intended to do so.

He listened, and then cautioned me. They have put you on the defensive, he said. You will spend your whole time denying the charges, and in so doing, no matter how persuasive your *argument,*

34. Magnuson-Moss Warranty Act, Pub. L. No. 93–637, 88 Stat. 2183 (1975).

you will still reinforce the defensive image of an agency responding to indictment by Congress.

"What you must do is to return to the specific cases of consumer injury, of human lives damaged, of families victimized by the practices which led to these commission proceedings. You have to rekindle the flame of public outrage. You have to redirect the focus from the commission to those industries and practices which victimized the consumer."

As I testified, I defended the commission as best I could; but then I did turn to cite the voices and the pain of real people who had been victimized in the marketplace. I told of a Connecticut woman, who had desperately sought an inexpensive cremation for her husband, forced to pay for a ruinously expensive casket because the funeral director falsely told her that an elaborate casket was legally required for cremation. I told of the victims of the misrepresentations of used car dealers; of a Los Angeles working woman who lost her savings and job by buying a cosmetically doctored wreck, soberly represented as sound and reliable transportation; of a seventy-nine-year-old Grand Rapids, Michigan, woman who was sold a hearing aid for $485 that did not work and in fact *could* not work, because her ear was clinically dead, yet the dealer refused to refund her money; of a small businessman from Connecticut who told our presiding officer that he was excluded from a major share of the market for his gauge equipment—though it was as good as, if not better than, its competitors—because the private, "voluntary" standard had been manipulated to force the sole use of his competitors' product.[35]

The committee were no longer listening.

There might have been just grounds for committee criticism of past commission implementation of its rule-making powers—and perhaps also for enjoining the commission to exercise caution before proposing new rules (though the commission was firmly committed to doing just that). But there was in the records of those oversight hearings nothing to justify the wholesale rewriting of the Federal Trade Commission Act.

The committee members enthusiastically embraced a crude rewriting of the basic FTC charter, the Federal Trade Commission Act,

35. See U.S., Congress, Senate, Committee on Commerce, *Oversight of the Federal Trade Commission*, 96th Congress, 1st sess., 1979, pp. 504–72.

which had stood for four decades essentially unchanged as a fundamental pillar of the nation's commitment to honesty and fair dealing
in the marketplace.

What had become of the "consumer movement" that had evoked
such loathing and fear in the collective Chambers of Commerce only
a decade earlier? Where were James Wilson's triumphant consumer
entrepreneurs of yesteryear?

Gone with the Berkeley Free Speech movement and fading
echoes, "blowin' in the wind"?

Not quite.

There still remained to be played out a second act to the "Perils of
the National Nanny," in which consumer advocacy did not quite
win out over its business and congressional tormentors, but did not
quite prove impotent either.

In the first scene of the second act, the National Nanny under-
goes a role change, learns better to play—and look—the part of
modest and law-abiding regulator, responsive public servant, arm
of Congress. Then a threadbare, but spirited and united, consumer/
labor coalition, led by the militant elderly, emerges to defend the
FTC. The media's indifference is finally breached by the venality of
the business lobbies and the supineness of Congress. Finally, in a
dramatic finale, the president, Jimmy Carter, faces down the congressional conferees in a confrontation set in the Theodore
Roosevelt room of the White House, just as the commission lies
gasping for appropriations.

But first the commission—and most especially its chairman—
had to redeem as best it could the consequences of its early political
imprudence and improve the dismal state of its congressional relations.

It had become painfully evident that the leadership that took
office in the spring of 1977 was afflicted with the chronic illusion of
omnipotence that seizes each new administration in turn (not least,
the present one).

In my own case, this illusory sense of political security, which
accompanied an equally illusory notion of a political mandate, was
compounded by the warm glow of my fourteen years as a faithful
servant of the Senate Commerce Committee, especially its powerful
and benign chairman, Senator Magnuson. I was also much im-
pressed with press accounts that cited, as among my undoubted
qualifications, manifest political skills and a network of warm Hill
relationships. As a consequence, we had at first turned to the task of

administering the Federal Trade Commission as if it were an independent agency.

As the Chinese poet/philosopher Laotzu chided, there are lessons we "know but never learn."[36] Heady with the scent of high office, I heard the siren call of Franklin Roosevelt proclaiming the independent agencies "tribunes of the people," champions of the public against "private greed."[37]

And I promptly forgot the heady power surges I had experienced as a staff member on the Senate Commerce Committee, forcing attentive and responsive commissioners and their emissaries to bend to the will of Congress as we shaped it, embodied for the moment in the then liberal majority of its oversight committees.

I knew, but hadn't learned, that the FTC served two masters—the public interest and the Congress. The public interest was a malleable absentee master, but the Congress held the whip.

And I did not fully comprehend that the former liberal and consumer-oriented Democratic majority of the Commerce Committee had been decimated by death, retirement, and election, and had been succeeded by a more conservative, or at least skittish, majority in a far more conservative political environment.

We had not taken the time to pay elementary respects to the members of the House Appropriations Committee and other congressional leaders and members in whose hands the commission's fate would rest.

And since we did not trouble to assure the congressmen and senators that our sole object in life was to carry out the will of Congress, the lawyer-lobbyists, the Washington business representatives, the local broadcasters, and other politically active businessmen were more than content to be left the task of characterizing this new commission leadership for the benefit of the members of Congress.

Their communications, unlike the commission's much maligned rule-making procedures, are not designed to present a balanced picture. When the lawyer-lobbyist comes around to his friends on the House Appropriations Committee to seek extraordinary action to deny funds for continuation of the commission's children's adver-

36. Witter Bynner, *The Way of Life According to Laotzu* (New York: John Day Co., 1944), p. 74.

37. Quoted in "Congressional Democratic Policy Statement on Regulatory Reform," paper presented to the White House, mimeographed, June 25, 1975.

tising rule-making inquiry, his need and purpose is to foment blind outrage, not balanced deliberation.

When Senator Danforth observes that "everywhere" he goes in Missouri, at "every Kiwanis or Rotary luncheon," he hears complaints about the Federal Trade Commission, this select constituency has formed his sense of the agency and its leadership.[38] And as congressmen compare notes with each other, an unflattering portrait emerges of an agency and its arrogant chairman, heedless and contemptuous of Congress.

The shaping of this image was not retarded by my own unfortunate tendency to untamed rhetoric in speeches and interviews. I had had the good sense not to make any speeches during the first four months of my chairmanship so that I might learn about the work of the commission before pronouncing upon it. It was a policy that, in retrospect, might fruitfully have been extended indefinitely. At least I might have tempered my rhetoric with humility and deference to Congress on the part of an unelected bureaucrat.

In November 1978, following the midterm congressional elections, and what was then perceived as the chill wind of conservatism, I paid a visit to Congressman Ben Rosenthal, chairman of the House Government Operations Committee's consumer subcommittee, a long-time consumer leader. The commission had already received an unexpected bruising at the hands of the appropriations subcommittee and the full House. I asked for counsel.

"Get up here," he said. "Let them see that you are not crazy. And it would help if you would make yourself a few friends—the House is a very personal place."

In the fall of 1978, we gathered together our full legislative liaison staff (it is not prudent for a public agency to refer to its legislative liaison staff as its lobbyists) to plot our legislative counter-offensive. Our numbers were not impressive: there were six of us, myself included.

The commission's general counsel was Mike Sohn, a former partner in the elegant Washington firm of Arnold and Porter, clear and forceful (and as forensically intimidating as any industry hired gun), strategically resourceful, and possessed of an uncommonly unyielding backbone.

---

38. U.S. Congress, Senate, Committee on Commerce, *Authorization for the FTC, Hearings before a Subcommittee of the Senate Committee on Commerce on S. 1020*, 96th Cong., 1st sess., 1979, p. 20.

Bill Baer, assistant general counsel for legislation (i.e., the chief lobbyist) was a deceptively youthful and disarming Stanford Law School graduate, who held a firm grasp of congressional motivations as well as the substance of the issues, and took wicked pleasure in disarming hostile congressmen and outflanking lobbyists.

Kathleen Sheekey was a former lobbyist for the Consumer Federation of America, disarming, ingratiating, keenly attuned to shifts in congressional winds. Though not a lawyer, Kathleen quickly earned the trust and respect of the commission's lawyers. Congressmen and their staffs just naturally wanted to help her.

Kevin Cronin, a lawyer who had worked on legislation with Esther Peterson (the president's consumer advisor), brought an informed anxiety to the group's deliberations. Through a network of Hill friendships and relationships, which he cultivated assiduously, Kevin was the preeminent intelligence gatherer, the first to sound the alarm. And he was an essential antidote to my own chronic Pollyanna-ish view of the world, especially Congress.

There was also Mark Lutes, a young student, who had not quite entered law school when he signed on for brief service as an intern with the legislative staff, and remained to spend months of fourteen- and fifteen-hour days in the commission's defense.

This was the commission's army of lobbyists. By comparison, the *Washington Star* reported that industries affronted by the children's advertising initiative alone had raised a "war chest" of fifteen to thirty million dollars to fight that proceeding.[39] One day, as I was gingerly comparing notes over the phone on the legislative situation with Tom Boggs, the industry's lobbying coordinator, Boggs offhandedly mentioned that he was scheduled to meet that very afternoon with representatives of thirty-two separate companies and associations banded together to prevent the regulation of children's advertising.

Our modest group shared a keen commitment to the commission's work, believing deeply in its justness. None of the staff were easily given to panic, at a time when panic would have been an appropriate response. But they also shared the lobbyist's professional delight in achieving intractable objectives through indirection, the lobbyist's preeminent skill at motivating both allies and bystanders to *want* to help, and a competitive instinct that refused to

---

39. Bailey Morris, "Foes of Child Ad Curbs Devised Strategy Here," *Washington Star*, March 7, 1979.

be intimidated by the vast array of lobbying resources available to business.

We shamelessly set about wooing Congress, day after day, week after week, starting the very day in December 1978 when new congressmen opened their offices to pay our respects to the new members (especially those who had expressed interest in our oversight committees). We laboriously courted the key members of the Commerce, Appropriations, Judiciary, Rules, and Small Business committees.

We learned to watch for trade association and congressional receptions at which we might be able to exchange civilities with ten, fifteen, or even twenty congressmen and their staffs in one setting. Early evenings were thus set aside for the cultivation of Congress, and in the early mornings there were frequent breakfasts in the House dining room. We did not confine these visits to potential supporters. It was at least equally important to meet with hostile members. We had learned that it is less pleasurable for a critical congressman to characterize as monstrous a bureaucrat with whom he has dined and discussed the foul state of Washington's weather, and one who has at least attempted to respond to his concerns or to those of his constituents.

I would not place too heavy an emphasis on the potential rewards of such "personal diplomacy." But these efforts did serve to vent some of the spleen of congressmen genuinely outraged at what they had been told of the commission's character.

And we took pride in contributing to some modest conversions. One such was Congressman Joseph Early (D) of Worcester, Massachusetts.

Joe Early is not a name that shakes the political firmament with the reverberations of a Kennedy or an O'Neill, but Congressman Joe Early of the Third District of Massachusetts, senior member of the House appropriations subcommittee on commerce, labor and justice, suddenly loomed very large and menacing in the path of the Federal Trade Commission in March 1979.

As we scanned the names of the members of the subcommittee in preparation for the hearing, we noted that Early was both a Democrat and from Massachusetts, a state noted for its liberal congressional delegation; we assumed he would be generally supportive of the commission and its programs. It was only one of a great number of such assumptions that I was to learn to regret.

To be sure, we had scheduled courtesy calls with the members of the subcommittee a few days before the hearing. With an unmistakable air of bureaucratic noblesse oblige, I made the rounds. The effort was transparently ingratiating and perfunctory. Congressman Early was pleasant enough, but not forthcoming; since it had taken me nearly two years to pay my respects, he had learned all he cared to know about the FTC elsewhere. He would see me at the hearing.

The hearing was an unrelievedly dismal event. I arrived with a supporting platoon of budget officers, counsel, program managers, administrators, buoyant with the self-important sense of mission befitting the chairman of a great regulatory agency. The subcommittee chairman was bored and distracted, which initiated my precipitous deflation. Like picadors, the Republican members delivered several skillfully inserted barbs and twisted them. But none of these preliminaries matched the venomous sarcasm and contempt that my appearance evoked from Congressman Early.

He began by suggesting that the commission's budgetary description of its work force in terms of "work years" (the feminist-inspired substitute for "man years") rather than number of positions was a crude fraud. I was utterly baffled by the arcane debate and, though our budget experts whispered explanations in my ear, the more I spoke, the more convinced Early evidently became that the documents before him bore all the earmarks of a surreptitious bureaucratic raid on the U.S. Treasury. He mocked, he scorned, and then he turned to the gravamen of his complaint: "The FTC doesn't do anything for consumers. All you ever do is promise, talk, and study. What has the FTC ever done to benefit the citizens of Worcester?"[40]

As I sputtered and struggled desperately to recall some dramatic consumer beneficence that the commission had bestowed on the citizens of Worcester, he rose with a gesture conveying eloquently the limits of tolerance breached and strode out of the hearing.

His absence improved matters only momentarily as the other committee members, stimulated by Early's example, returned to the attack with reverberating ferocity.

I lay awake that night seeking an appropriate scheme of venge-

40. U.S. Congress, House, Committee on Appropriations, *Departments of State, Justice, and Commerce, the Judiciary, and Related Agencies Appropriations for 1980* 96th Cong., 1st sess., 1979, pp. 774–75.

ance, but by dawn had grasped again the essential principle that it
never pays to arouse a senior member of one's appropriations subcommittee. And so, instead, the next morning we set about reclaim-
ing the heart and mind of Joe Early.

We made discreet inquiries with staff members of the Massachusetts delegation and learned, somewhat to our surprise, that while
Early was a notorious fiscal curmudgeon, he was widely viewed as
fair (though skeptical), very hard-working, and fiercely independent of the Speaker, as well as of lobbyists. We also learned, though,
that Early had been visited by his friend Tom Boggs, who in addition
to being the son of a former House majority leader was a prominent
Democratic fund-raiser and disarming champion of the sugar,
broadcast, and cereal interests.

We sent for a three-day supply of the *Worcester Telegram* and
poured through its pages studying the ads (including the classi-
fieds) until we had identified fifteen specimens of advertising
that bore tangible evidence of the benefits to Worcester citizens of
commission actions. (They included discounts on Levi's, which
could not have occurred until the commission challenged Levi
Strauss's retail price-fixing policies; and price discounts and competition among optometrists, which had been avoided by the self-reg-
ulatory schemes of the optometrists until the commission challenged such prohibitions as unfair restraints on competition.)

I wrote a long, deferential letter to Congressman Early, citing the
FTC-inspired improvements reflected in each of these ads and the
tangible benefits flowing therefrom to Worcester citizens. We
learned later that he was pleased with the letter (and, since congressmen are accustomed to receiving computer-customized letters
from the great federal bureaucracies, he was *especially* pleased at the
assurances by our congressional relations staff that I had really written it myself).

Through a mutual friend, I wheedled an invitation to the annual
St. Patrick's Day stag party given by lawyer Paul McGowen to honor
Speaker O'Neill and his friends. I went and drank green beer to the
health of every member of the Massachusetts delegation.

I had only a brief opportunity to exchange pleasantries with Joe
Early, but had the great good fortune to meet Jim Shannon, a
shrewd, committed young congressman from Lowell, Mass., who
uttered rare and welcome words of support and encouragement for
the commission's work. I told him of our earlier travails with Joe
Early, and he readily volunteered to arrange a dinner for the three of

us in which I could add my own strokes to Tom Boggs's lopsided portrait of the commission—and at the same time show myself to be possibly human.

Kathleen Sheekey sought out Congressman Early's key staff people, especially those who followed the commission for him. She kept them alert to commission activities that affected their constituents, and through them stayed attuned to their concerns and to any negative tremors generated by constituents or peripatetic lobbyists.

And our Boston regional director, Lois Pines, initiated a lively and successful small business conference in Worcester, designed to let small businessmen vent their frustrations and sense of helplessness to the dreaded regulators in person—an event Congressman Early could comfortably co-sponsor and appropriately take credit for as a forum for decrying the dangers of insensitive or unduly burdensome regulations.

In 1980 the House subcommittee on state, justice, and commerce held its annual appropriation hearing for the FTC. A chastened and respectful FTC chairman cited extensive evidence of the commission's sensitivity to, and responsiveness to, the concerns of this subcommittee and of the Congress. Congressman Early responded first:

> I have been a critic of some of the FTC activities in the past, but I [now] believe much of what the agency does is of value to the public. . . . Any regulatory agency is supposed to be controversial and if controversy is doing a good job, you are our Eric Heiden. I believe you are going in the right direction. . . . I am particularly impressed with your regulatory analysis. You have been sensitive to unnecessary and overly burdensome regulation without compromising the public's interest. . . . The job you are doing with your limited budget is important and the right way to go.[41]

THE CONSUMER-LABOR COALITION

But such agency self-help could, at best, serve limited objectives.

Congressman Early and a few other members, when exposed to both sides of the issues, did make an effort to weigh them fairly. They were prepared to listen, and took pride in preserving their

41. U.S. Congress, House, Committee on Appropriations, *Departments of State, Justice, and Commerce, the Judiciary, and Related Agencies Appropriations for 1981.* 96th Cong., 2d sess., 1980, pp. 150–51.

independence from the lobbyists. Most did not. Indeed many
House members made commitments to the first business advocate
through their door. Former Congressman John Murphy of New
York told me after listening sympathetically to my arguments in
support of the extreme modesty and rationality of our funeral rule,
"Well, we're gonna give this one to Marty [Russo] as a going-away
present [from the House Commerce Committee]." Congressman
Russo had just been appointed to the Ways & Means Committee.

Other members were equally candid. I called upon an old friend,
a good liberal, who had gone down the line with the commission in
past battles. "I was afraid you would ask me that," he said. "Ask me
anything else. For ten years my campaign treasurer has been a
leading funeral director in the state. I can't help you. I won't talk,
and I'll vote late, but that is all I can do."

Another congressman explained the pressures he was feeling
this way:

> You know a funeral director can kill you, I go to forty or fifty funerals a
> year. He decides whether you sit next to the widow or at the back of
> the room and when you're at a funeral parlor for one funeral and
> there's another one going on, a friendly funeral director introduces
> you to the family. The funeral directors have got a lot of time. . . . They
> are big joiners. They join the Kiwanis, the Rotaries, and they are very
> active in the community; then everybody knows them.

No matter how persuasive our later arguments might have been,
they came too late. We might change their *minds*, but not their *votes*.

Because agency advocacy consists in substantial measure of the
display of agency deference, by its very nature it cannot be dele-
gated by the agency's chief executive to staff. It thus quickly runs up
against the physical limitations of one person's time and energy. At
best, with dogged effort, we had made modest progress toward
counteracting the effects of our own neglect. We would never rank
high among any congressman's favorite agencies (especially since
we made no grants, contracted for little more than paper and pen-
cils, and gave mostly pain to constituent businessmen). But at least
we had taken the raw edge off congressional antipathy.

After the vote by the Senate Commerce Committee in October,
but well before the Senate floor debate on the FTC-proposed
amendments in February 1980, we attempted to meet with as many
Senate members as possible, and paid equal court to key Senate staff

members, who tend to play a more central role in the shaping of Senate attitudes than their House counterparts.

By the time of the full Senate debate, the attacks on the commission, though hardly lacking in enthusiasm, at least focused on substantive issues. Largely absent was the harsh and personal demonology that had characterized the earlier House floor debates.

But we could have made passionate love to Congress twenty-four hours a day and still have been swept along in the anti-regulatory tidal wave. By the fall of 1979 or the spring of 1980, it should have been plain to even an amateur Congress-watcher that any bill or amendment that bore the label of regulatory reform or, perhaps more appropriate, of "regulatory revolt," would carry the House by a two-to-one vote, the Senate by a three-to-two vote.

To be sure, there remained in both Houses remnants of consumer leadership. The House Commerce Committee retained a fortuitously disproportionate core of unreconstructed consumer advocates, both members and staff, among them the chairman of the consumer subcommittee, James Scheuer. He and his small, but spirited, entrepreneurial staff were to be pressed almost beyond endurance by the lobbyists and their congressional supporters, but they would not yield. And, by their resourcefulness, they more than once converted pending disaster to advantage.[42] There were supportive members of the Senate, too, perhaps none so committed or so prepared to spend unflagging energy in defense of consumer rights as Howard Metzenbaum of Ohio. And it was energy, more than votes, that was in shortest supply, though there were a handful of others, like Bob Packwood of Oregon, who would be supportive and willing to take the lead in defense of specific proceedings.

For the commission to emerge essentially undiminished, a reprise of entrepreneurial politics was indeed essential. And it did

---

42. The subcommittee staff, newly selected by Chairman Scheuer, did not have much prior FTC experience. But each staffer enthusiastically brought his own set of talents to the fight. Staff director Ed Rovner drew upon his substantial Hill experience and his detailed knowledge of the motives and characters of the critical members. In his job for only a few months when the FTC reauthorization fight began, subcommittee staffer George Kopp quickly became a key consumer entrepreneur. Armed with information, and respected by all sides, his instincts for timing and potential compromise strategies helped to shape the eventual salvage of the FTC. Jonah Shacknai, Congressman Scheur's staffer, contributed astute political sense to the fray, and Peter Kinzler, Kopp's predecessor, provided historical perspectives on prior FTC fights and issues.

take place, largely because the two other key elements of the earlier entrepreneurial politics survived, though diminished: skillful consumer advocates and a responsive press.

With Congressman Scheuer and his staff and Evelyn Dubrow, the tiny—and fierce—lobbyist for the International Ladies Garment Workers Union, as catalysts, the consumer advocates drew together in an informal coalition whose working title was only slightly less overbearing than the Chamber of Commerce's counterpart coalition of "victims of the FTC," the Consumer/Labor Coalition to Save the FTC.

In the past, consumer advocates had not readily joined forces in defense of a regulatory agency. Indeed, much of their most successful work had consisted of condemnatory assaults on the various regulatory agencies, including the FTC. Their level of trust in any government agency was generally about as high as their confidence in the public-interest commitment of General Motors. In this case, however, Congress brought us together. One benign by-product of the intemperate attacks by business and its congressional spokesmen on the commission was their utility in convincing consumer representatives that the FTC was indeed worth saving.

The coalition contained few new entrants, but displayed the enthusiasm and the teamwork characteristic of embattled allies "back to back in a knife fight." There was the Consumer Federation of America, of course, but without Carol Foreman (who had become Carter's assistant secretary of agriculture for consumer affairs), and Congress Watch, but without Joan Claybrook (who had become Carter's national highway traffic safety administrator). With a number of "workers" (lobbyists prepared to spend at least some time "working the Congress"), the coalition drew its greatest support from organized labor (perhaps ten or twelve representatives at any given time). It is, of course, fashionable to decry the petrification of idealism in the mature labor movement. But the fact is that the labor lobbyists brought a deep sense of commitment to a task that was, after all, theoretically secondary to their principal institutional responsibility to defend against direct encroachment on workers' rights and economic well-being. Mike Gildea, a young assistant to the chief lobbyist for the AFL–CIO, served as principal coordinator for the coalition with a generous and selfless spirit that infused the work of the group—a quality rare enough among the not infrequent jealousies and petty rivalries (both institutional and personal) that afflict the world of the Washington lobbyist, profit and non-profit alike. And they were joined by groups representing the organized voice of the nation's elderly—the National Council of Senior Citizens, traditionally the most aggressive advocate for the elderly, and the increasingly militant American Association of Retired Persons.

The elderly were, not unsurprisingly, most deeply concerned about congressional efforts to strike down the funeral-price disclosure rule, but there were also a number of other commission initiatives that had convinced the leadership of these organizations that the FTC provided a first line of defense against economic exploitation of the elderly. Perhaps most important, for a large majority of the elderly, *consumer* issues—defending purchasing power and the integrity of the marketplace in which they buy—replace wage and income enhancement issues as the primary economic concern. Among them are many who are informed and active, often drawing upon the mature skills of past professional life. They have the time and motivation to shop carefully, and are therefore among those consumers most able to take advantage of mandated information disclosure and truthful price comparisons. In self-defense against the ravages of inflation, they have become increasingly militant in the political defense of their economic rights.

The coalition served to shore up the hemorrhaging support on the Hill for the commission. To those members of Congress inclined to support the commission, they provided reassurance that there was at least modest institutional support for that position. For those congressmen and senators inclined to support their business constituents, but not deeply committed to the FTC legislation as a jihad against the heathen regulators, the coalition served for the first time to suggest that other constituents than business cared about the fate of the FTC, and that others were watching.

After the House vote to kill the funeral rule, the elderly, in particular, began to write their congressmen, not in inundating volume, but in sufficient numbers and with such evident spontaneity and genuineness of outrage that legislators began to sense that a vote for their friendly local funeral director might not be entirely without cost.

But despite its working harmony and commitment, the coalition simply lacked sufficient lobbying leverage to reverse the anti-regulatory sentiment. The coalition first came together in an all-out, unified effort to defeat the Russo amendment vetoing the funeral rule on the House floor, in October 1979. Although the coalition was active and aggressive in the days preceding the House vote, the amendment had not yet attracted significant media attention, and the coalition had not had time to help stimulate the expression of grassroots concern by the day of the vote. Ironically, their lobbying efforts against the funeral amendment were actively supported by a number of lobbyists for other business interests, such as the coalition against the children's advertising proceeding, which (correctly) saw the funeral rule as adding risky, politically charged negative freight to the FTC bill, perhaps endangering the whole. Despite this unlikely coalition, the amendment passed by a two-to-one margin.

The commission's own role as participant in the consumer/labor coalition remained necessarily vague and delicate. When it comes to lobbying Congress, agencies, like small children, are expected to speak only when questioned. Direct lobbying—that is, the use of appropriated funds directly to influence Congress—is barred by criminal statute.[43] Though no one has been prosecuted in the sixty-year history of that statute, it does tend to chill the more aggressive agency efforts to generate support. (Viewers of the Defense Department's relationship with defense contractors and Congress may be surprised to learn of its existence.)

Still, in the best of all possible worlds, bureaucrats ought not to be spending the taxpayers' money to justify their powers or existence. Moreover, to be perceived as lobbying certainly tends to undercut the very legitimacy of the agency's effort to portray itself as a humble and dutiful public servant responding to the will of Congress.

But we did have a key role to play for the coalition. Kathleen Sheekey, especially, universally trusted from her days as a lobbyist for the Consumer Federation, coordinated its communications, making certain that each member of the coalition was (and felt) informed of legislative developments and even individual congressional tremors.

The commission staff, who were the only truly expert resource available to the coalition, were called upon to provide "appropriate material" responsive to congressional and other inquiries. And we participated as a full, if silent, partner in shaping the coalition's strategy.

The essential strategic task was plain. The coalition had to develop a media strategy to generate and stimulate critical attention to the congressional effort to "cripple" the commission—the more outraged and intemperate the better. For the more raucous media

43. 18 *U.S. Code* §1913 (1976).

attention could be focused on the essential corruption of the legislative process, the less stomach Congress's more skittish and weakly committed members would have for pressing forward with the dismantling of commission proceedings. A strong showing of diverse media support for the commission would equally serve to demonstrate to the White House, especially to the president's political advisors, that defense of the Federal Trade Commission, even in a time of apparently prevailing anti-regulatory sentiment, was a popular cause.

The coalition found itself possessed of certain media assets, among them the pungency of the funeral-rule amendment. We had been perhaps insufficiently grateful at the time, but the Russo amendment proved to have been an unintended political gift. It simply would not go down quietly.

Paul Turley, the director of the commission's Chicago regional office (who had come to the commission via the ministry), is uncommonly sensitive to the real-world concerns and attitudes of consumers. He remarked to me shortly after House adoption of the Russo amendment, that *no* consumer issue evoked from general audiences such spontaneous support as the funeral rule—or such spontaneous outrage as the amendment to kill the rule. He contrasted that reaction with his audience's more ambivalent response to the commission's effort to police misrepresentations in used car sales. While it is true that, justly or not, consumers have lower confidence in the representations of used car salesmen than almost any other trade, many believe that their own familiarity with, and wariness of, the used car trade arms them to defend themselves. But the same consumers understand full well that the unique and debilitating circumstances of funeral transactions leave them naked to exploitation. Even the arch-conservative Heritage Foundation, in its transition blueprint to the new Reagan administration for the dismantling of government (especially regulation), found favor with the commission's funeral rule. Its report concluded: "[As there] is no effective or adequate marketplace remedy available to a bereaved family when a funeral home refuses to provide them with an itemized bill, or when it induces them to purchase an unwanted package of goods and services, . . . the issuance of prohibiting trade regulatory rules is justified."[44]

---

44. Kendell Fleeharty, "Federal Trade Commission," in *Mandate for Leadership: Policy Management in a Conservative Administration,* edited by Charles L. Heatherly (Washington, D.C.: The Heritage Foundation, 1981), p. 766.

In shaping the final funeral rule, the commission had, moreover, performed its tasks carefully and prudently, pruning the regulation down to its bare essentials: truth and the simple requirement of an itemized price list.

Fairly or unfairly, the funeral director is not to be found among favored American role models. Such devastating critiques of funeral practices as Jessica Mitford's *The American Way of Death* and the Evelyn Waugh novel *The Loved One* (translated into a popular film) augmented the faintly disreputable public aura surrounding the industry, despite funeral directors' desperate reach for respectability as professional "grief counselors."

And, while undertakers have their own peculiar advantage in achieving political access, they, unlike cereal manufacturers, do little advertising either in newspapers or on the broadcast affiliates of newspaper conglomerates.

The coalition developed three core media themes:

1. Reinforcement of the image of the commission as dutiful public servant. The commission was only carrying out the earlier expressed will of Congress.

2. The *lawlessness* of congressional interference with trials, inquiries, and proceedings being faithfully carried out by the commission under due process established by the Congress itself. It was Mike Sohn, the commission's general counsel, who argued persuasively that the commission's most politically potent argument rested upon the *illegitimacy* of congressional interference with pending trials and administrative proceedings. This argument unmasked congressmen so eager to do the bidding of lobbyists that they could not restrain themselves until the commission or the courts had dealt with, and perhaps resolved, their concerns. It sidestepped the necessarily elaborate, and perhaps diversionary, defense of the merits of each of the several proceedings under attack.

This strategic theme had the added virtue of disarming those White House staff members who had displayed discomfort with the children's advertising initiative and gave indications of a readiness to sacrifice it as legislative ballast. It also left room for the commission's allies to espouse individual proceedings, such as the funeral rule, whose virtues were readily communicated, but did not require that the commission's supporters defend or endorse the substance of each and every threatened rule proposal.

3. The struggle between the forces of light and the usual villains: the insidious business lobbyists and their toadies in Congress. Long a mainstay of consumer, environmental, and other public-interest entrepreneurial politics, the theme of lobbying villainy retained its vitality, as was demonstrated by opinion polls that showed that while there might be a growing *minority* concerned about over-regulation, an overwhelming *majority* of the American public were troubled by the perceived pernicious influence of business on government decision making.

There were the generic lobbies to condemn. "The funeral lobby," "the cigarette lobby," "the sugar lobby," "the cereal lobby," "the broadcast lobby," "the used car lobby," and the "learned" professional lobbies, such as the American Medical Association, were closely associated in legislative tradition with mean-spirited causes.

And there were the individual lobbyists, who served to personify the back-door manipulation of the legislative process, the undemocratic influence of economic power and privilege, and the unwholesome link between generous campaign funding sources and votes supportive of industry.

There was Tom Boggs, the son of the former House majority leader, a virtuoso lawyer lobbyist and a principal fund-raiser for the Democratic senatorial campaign committee headed by Wendell Ford, chairman of the consumer subcommittee.

There was John Filer, president of AETNA and the American Council on Life Insurance, a friend of the president and leader of Businessmen for Carter, whose firm had delivered to the Senate Commerce Committee members an artful, if disingenuous, brief "establishing" the commission's illegitimacy in conducting its study of life insurance cost disclosure.

Even Wilbur Mills appeared in a cameo role in the Commerce Committee oversight hearings, sitting, in deference to congressional protocol, on the dais with the committee members and staff, while lobbying for *Encyclopaedia Britannica*.

Throughout October and November 1979, we alternated between gloomy resignation and panic. The appropriations committees were threatening to withhold all funding from the commission until an authorization bill had been enacted.

The House version of the FTC's authorization bill contained a one-house legislative veto provision for all future FTC rules, a provision excising the commission's authority to challenge generic trademarks (the Formica amendment)[45] and amendments terminating the commission's funeral rule and monopolization case against the Sunkist agricultural cooperative.

The Senate Commerce Committee's coyly mislabeled "FTC Improvements Act" bestowed legislative indulgences upon the life insurance industry, the broadcasters and their allies in children's advertising, the cigarette advertisers, and the industries who sought to avoid FTC scrutiny of the voluntary standards process.

In November 1979, Congress adjourned before the Senate had taken up the Commerce Committee's "FTC Improvements Act." By then we were convinced that only a "media blitz" could save the commission from dismemberment once Congress reconvened in January 1980.

As obnoxious as were the Senate Commerce Committee FTC amendments, there were growing signs that when the Senate reconvened and took up the bill, virtually every other business that found an FTC proceeding uncongenial would find willing Senate sponsorship for a remedial amendment. Indeed the staff of the Republican steering committee (entrepreneurially pursuing their own vision of economic libertarianism) had extended a blanket invitation to business through the Chamber of Commerce and other conservative organizations to come forward with private business relief amendments, for which the committee staff volunteered to find enthusiastic sponsorship.

For if the cereal companies and life insurance industry had found legislative relief at the hands of the Commerce Committee, who, in fairness, could deny freedom from FTC vexation to the doctors, dentists, lawyers, mobile home manufacturers, used car dealers, funeral directors, over-the-counter drug manufacturers, and so on?

The labor and consumer organization members of the coalition engaged in open and aggressive efforts to gain access to the media, such as the flamboyant press conference at the Capitol two weeks before the House vote on the Russo funeral amendment, which

45. Section 14 of the Lanham Trademark Act of 1946, 15 U.S.C. §1064, directs the FTC to challenge trademarks that have passed into the public realm as generic terms (like aspirin, cellophane, thermos bottles, linoleum, etc.). In 1978 the commission petitioned the Trademark Trial and Appeals Board challenging the Formica trademark. By enhancing competition through ending the Formica Company's monopoly over the use of the term Formica, the result would have been to allow other manufacturers of plastic laminates to compete in the market for Formica, which surveys show most consumers believe is indeed the generic term for plastic laminates.

included Esther Peterson and Bess Myerson, representatives of the elderly, and congressional and consumer leaders. While this and other efforts were too late to evoke a sufficient public response to affect that particular vote, they contributed to the growing media portrait of a Congress toadying to the lobbies.

At the FTC, our own contribution was in a lower key, and necessarily less visible. But it was no less energetic. Through our press office, we made certain that factual background documents reached the hands of any reporter, columnist, or editorial writer who might wish to be informed about the commission's plight. Meanwhile, the coalition circulated joint letters and statements less circumspectly denouncing Congress and the business lobbies. Though I was amply employed at the commission, I found time to call columnists and editorial writers.

But not reporters. For some time it had been the unflattering consensus of my colleagues at the commission that a silent, if not invisible, chairman was the most potent antidote to the image of an intemperate, biased commission leadership.

My posture toward Congress had to be one of chastened submissiveness, not the stuff of successful press conferences; besides, a statement from the commander of the Alamo portraying it as the lone, heroic, embattled outpost of virtue would be unseemly (and unconvincing).

There were consumer advocates with access to the media, such as Senator Metzenbaum, Congressman Eckhart and Congressman Scheuer, who performed heroic, sometimes lonely, service in defense of principle and the FTC in Congress. They were not only articulate and forceful, but spoke with legitimacy, as elected people's representatives, not unelected bureaucrats. The public defense of the commission was best left to others.

This rule was partially breached (though not without misgivings) for several television opportunities. A potentially sympathetic segment of "60 Minutes" recounting the commission's trials and tribulations was in the offing, which would not go forward unless I agreed to participate. Ralph Nader had also urged me to accept an invitation to appear on the "Phil Donahue Show," while Bill Moyers was exploring a one-hour documentary on the commission and its adversaries. To the skeptical among us, I swore to abjure such outbursts as my vow back in the days of self-righteous defiance that Congress would have "to break my arm" before I would yield on the children's advertising issue. I would conform to an unwavering posture of injured innocence and humility—a humility, I may add, that at that point in my tenure was both genuine and earned.

The press response was a rolling barrage of critical editorials, fortunately aimed not at the FTC but at Congress. Beginning with the *Washington Post, Washington Star, New York Times, Philadelphia Inquirer,* and *Los Angeles Times,* it was echoed by nearly a hundred editorials throughout the country in papers as philosophically and geographically diverse as the *Honolulu Star Bulletin* and the *Charleston Gazette* (West Virginia).[46]

In January, February, and March 1980 there followed several major television programs on the conflict. The "Phil Donahue Show" proved a remarkable experience. Donahue, a great showman, respects his audience of eight million—mostly women at home. He was not entirely sympathetic. Indeed, as I began to warm to the friendly response of the studio audience (especially reacting to the funeral directors' lobbying efforts), and began to expand confidently on the virtues of the FTC, Donahue punctured my euphoria with a quick series of informed, troublesome questions. To avoid the charge that I was engaging in illicit lobbying efforts, I encouraged Donahue's viewers to let their Congressmen know their feelings "no matter *which* side you're on."

The program evoked several thousand supportive letters to the commission and Congress. That is not, of course, an avalanche of mail compared to the modern norm for organized letter-writing campaigns. But even a dozen thoughtful and spontaneous letters might give pause to a congressman who could say, prior to the House vote on the Russo amendment, that he had never heard from a single constituent in support of the commission.

Bill Moyers, not surprisingly, offered the most thoughtful and probing analysis. But "60 Minutes," the Big Bertha of public-affairs programming, had a truly transformative impact.[47]

While both "60 Minutes" and "Bill Moyers' Journal" gave me an opportunity to defend the commission, it was the eloquent self-portrait of Congress in film and tape clips of Commerce Committee members championing one special economic interest after another in self-righteous high dudgeon and the fatuousness of much of the

46. Senator Howard Metzenbaum placed many of these editorials in the *Congressional Record,* 96th Cong., 2d sess., February 6, 1980, 126, no. 17: 1053–73.
47. CBS, *Wild to Regulate,* "60 Minutes," February 3, 1980.

House funeral debate that served to strip the veil of regulatory reform from the congressional posturing.

The portrait of the conflict that emerged in the print and broadcast media was not flattering to Congress. The commission was seen not as the "National Nanny," but as the honest cop on the consumer beat, punished for daring to question powerful economic interests. What had earlier been portrayed by critics as an arrogant, zealous chairman and commission now appeared as an earnest and responsive watchdog, notable for its temerity in taking on the special interests; reasonable, but unyielding and unrepentant; modest, not arrogant; an agency taking to heart the tasks assigned to it by that very Congress.

Instead of as the Tyrannosaurus rex of the regulatory agencies, the FTC was portrayed by cartoonists, especially Herblock, as hat in hand, head slightly bent, standing humbly before congressional inquisitors who held the commission "guilty of acting like a regulatory agency"; or as the pathetic victim of the torturer's lash ("Still want to help all those common people?") Perhaps most painful to the pride of the congressmen involved was Herblock's caricature of the Congress as a ventriloquist's dummy in the lap of the special interests.[48]

"Sixty Minutes" aired a little over a week before the Senate debate on the FTC Bill. That debate was scheduled to begin on Thursday, the very day that President Carter had tentatively agreed to appear before the "Consumer Assembly," the annual gathering of consumer and labor organizations in Washington. Our strategy and our lobbying of the White House was designed to stimulate a firm and timely presidential veto threat.

We had enjoyed strong support from Esther Peterson, the president's consumer advisor, an old and true ally, and from the president's domestic advisor, Stuart Eizenstat. We had enjoyed uncommon support from the president himself. But we knew also that the president was in the midst of a bitter primary campaign and that his political advisors would in large measure determine the extent of his involvement.

We had forwarded a steady stream of favorable editorials and clippings to every White House staff member who might have some say in shaping the president's speech. We had been striking a responsive chord in the White House, but "60 Minutes" galvanized

48. *Washington Post*, November 30, 1979; December 26, 1979; May 2, 1980.

White House staff support for both the president's appearance and an unequivocal stand in support of the commission. As Ann Wexler, the president's counselor for political affairs, commented the day after "60 Minutes" ran: "When the president speaks about the FTC, forty million people will know what he is talking about, who until this week had barely heard of the FTC."

The drafts of the president's consumer assembly speech grew progressively stronger. Indeed he added emphasis himself, and he received from that otherwise tepid audience a standing ovation when he vowed "to veto any bill which would cripple the FTC."[49]

One industry lobbyist with whom I talked that week acknowledged that congressional sentiment for punishing the FTC had "peaked." Indeed, when the Senate took up the FTC bill, the stack of special-interest amendments that had been pending for weeks to stop those cases or proceedings not already targeted for extinction in the Commerce Committee bill were either withdrawn or defeated. There was a spirited, though losing, fight on behalf of the Magnuson-Packwood amendment to preserve the children's advertising and standards proceedings.

The committee leadership also faced a floor challenge by Senator Metzenbaum and others to the committee's determination that the commission should undertake *no* studies of insurance industry abuses. These amendments failed (as we expected they would, since the Commerce Committee and its leadership were united in opposing all amendments) though the commission's authority to complete its "medi-gap insurance study" was restored.

The tenor of the Senate debate was far removed from that of the House. There were strong words of support for the commission and attacks on the special-interest aroma of the Commerce Committee bill. The committee leaders, especially Ford and Danforth, were defensive throughout the debate.

For the next three months, the fate of the legislation rested in the hands of a Senate-House Conference Committee. In the beginning there was strong sentiment among a majority of the House conferees for dropping all special-interest amendments for a compromise that would impose some form of legislative veto on commission rule making, though there was potential deadlock on the issue of whether such a legislative veto could be exercised by only one

49. U.S., President, *Public Papers of the President of the United States* (Washington, D.C., Office of the *Federal Register,* National Archives and Records Service, 1953–), p. 282 (Speech before the Consumer Federation of America, February 7, 1980).

body, as in the House-passed bill, or had to be voted by both. Even conservative members, such as North Carolina Republican James Broyhill, had become uneasy with media challenges to the legitimacy of congressional interference with ongoing cases and rulemaking proceedings.

Senator Wendell Ford, the de facto chairman of the Senate conferees was not, however, prepared to yield. He had consistently opposed a legislative veto, but favored direct action by Congress to restrict the commission's activities. And he believed that he could forge an alliance among industry groups. He reasoned that if the conference committee adopted every special-interest amendment contained in either House or Senate bill, the combined political support of groups favoring each of these provisions would furnish sufficient votes either to intimidate the president or override any veto.

Crucial to Ford's control of the Senate conferees was Senator Danforth, the ranking Republican member of the committee, whom Ford had carefully and deliberately involved as a partner in the shaping of the Senate bill.

Danforth was stung by the press characterization of the legislation. He carried around with him one of the Herblock cartoons, as published in the *St. Louis Post-Dispatch*. He was open, he said, to reasonable compromise. But Senator Ford held him fast to their joint venture, and the compromise that would have preserved the commission's proceedings faded.

Enter, again, Ralph Nader. In a series of forays into Kentucky and Missouri, stimulating consumer groups and directly attacking Ford and Danforth, Nader was neither subtle nor reasonable in characterizing the conflict. Nor did he try to be. Attacking Ford in Kentucky, Nader cited a recent tragic fire in which more than a hundred people were burned. One theory was that the fire had been caused by aluminum wiring. Testimony before the commission in its voluntary standards proceeding had shown that the standard-setting process that had approved the uses of aluminum wiring had been so dominated by the aluminum industry as to preclude adequate consideration of the hazards of aluminum. Nader was careful not to directly accuse Ford of causing the fire; but a story that appeared in the *Kentucky Post* was not so punctilious.[50]

---

50. Joseph P. Shapiro, "Bill Guts Testing of Aluminum Wiring," *Kentucky Post*, February 8, 1980, p. 1.

In Missouri the *St. Louis Post-Dispatch* had focused editorial attention on Danforth as the critical vote in determining whether the FTC would be crippled.[51] Nader and the Missouri Public Interest Research Group, an affiliated consumer advocacy organization, attacked Danforth, citing the apparent conflict of interest between Danforth's votes undermining the commission's children's advertising proceeding and his inherited economic interest in Ralston Purina, an advertiser of children's cereals.

Ford and Danforth cried foul. Ford called me, consumed with indignation that Nader could suggest an association between his opposition to the standards proceeding and the death of 138 Kentuckyans. I felt compelled to issue a statement decrying as unfair any suggestion that Ford's position on standards could have contributed to the fire.

Wendell Ford believed, told all who would listen, and doubtless believes to this day that I directed Nader in every word and deed and that I could snap my fingers and produce nationwide editorials. It was hardly pleasant to be the target of such congressional wrath. Yet despite Ford's threats of vengeance, these illusions of our power to manipulate the media served as one of the very few deterrents in our efforts to restrain the Ford strategy of forging a coalition of corporate "victims" of the FTC.

Danforth was also outraged. He considered Nader's assertion that his votes were related to his family wealth and connections to Ralston Purina unjust and unfounded attacks upon his integrity. He resented the cartoonists' caricatures of himself and his colleagues as compliant handymen for corporate lobbyists. (Indeed, Danforth *had* strongly defended the commission's antitrust authority.) I have no doubts that these sentiments were genuine. I am equally certain

---

51. On April 1, 1980, the *St. Louis Post-Dispatch* ran an editorial entitled "Special Interest Leash for the FTC," which stated in part: "A Senate-House conference committee is completing work on a bill that, depending on its final form, will determine whether the Federal Trade Commission will be crippled in its efforts to protect consumers. Under heavy lobbying pressure from business interests, both houses passed bills aimed at curbing the FTC's power. . . . As a member of the conference committee, Missouri's Senator Danforth has an opportunity to stand up for consumers or to do the work of the special interests by undercutting the FTC's authority." Nine days later, another *Dispatch* editorial stated: "As the ranking Republican on a Senate-House conference committee, Missouri's Senator Danforth will have a crucial role in determining whether the committee reports a bill that destroys the Federal Trade Commission's power to protect consumers. . . . Senator Danforth, who posed as a champion of consumer interests when he was Missouri attorney general, now has a chance to demonstrate whose side he is on."

that these attacks caused Danforth for the first time to pause to view the FTC legislation from a perspective other than that of the Kiwanis and Chamber of Commerce, the complaining companies and industries.

On April 24th, Carter invited the conferees to the White House. Ford opened the meeting by complaining to the president that the personal attacks on him by Ralph Nader had caused him sleepless nights, and that "there isn't going to be any FTC if Ralph Nader is not turned off." The president, who had himself been the increasingly frequent target of Nader's outrage, replied with a wan smile, "You know I don't control Ralph Nader." The president then spelled out his bottom line, issue by issue, and he promised that a bill that fell below that line in any of its particulars would be vetoed. The Senate conferees backed down.[52]

CONCLUSION

The funeral-price disclosure rule proceeding was allowed to continue essentially unobstructed. The commission's antitrust case against Sunkist would go forward. The children's advertising proceeding would theoretically be allowed to continue, to the extent that the practices involved came within the confines of deception law, but not the commission's broader general authority to bar "unfair" practices. The standards and certification proceeding was allowed to continue in modified, but significant, form. Only our lone petition to cancel the Formica trademark failed utterly to escape congressional interment. The commission was permitted to undertake future insurance studies (but only at the request of a majority of either Senate or House Commerce Committee) and to complete its study of so-called medigap abuses. Commission rules henceforward would be subject to congressional veto, but only upon action by a majority of both houses of Congress. We rejoiced. The National Nanny had emerged from the crucible with her basic faculties, if not her pride, intact.

That night, we gathered around a TV set to watch the evening news accounts of the White House meeting—and witnessed a stunning event.

52. The conference version of the "Federal Trade Commission Improvements Act of 1980" was passed by the House on May 20, 1980, by a vote of 272 (Yeas) to 127 (Nays) and passed the Senate the next day by 74 (Yeas) to 15 (Nays).

The conference committee leaders, Senators Cannon and Ford and Congressman Staggers, emerged from the conference with the president and mounted the White House press podium to announce the compromise with appropriate pomp and sanctimony.

A reporter asked what precisely would be the impact of the suspension of the commission's authority over unfair advertising. Cannon and Ford hesitated momentarily. Suddenly Senator Robert Packwood, the ranking Republican member of the Commerce Committee shouldered his way to the microphone: "I'll tell you what stopping the commission's unfairness authority means," he said bitterly: "You're going to have a generation of kids with rotten teeth and cancerous lungs because of this bill; henceforth any ad that is unfair, alluring, any ad directed at our children that you can't prove is false is going to be allowed."

"Three principal groups want this bill changed—the advertising industry itself, sugar, and tobacco. They're getting their way."[53]

Senators Cannon and Ford melted away, and Packwood's outrage chilled our own short-lived euphoria too. Subdued, we reflected on the lessons we had learned from our bruising legislative journey. There were precious few grounds for rejoicing.

True, toward the end we had succeeded in narrowing the lobbying gap between us and our business adversaries. Most important, with the unyielding support of the president, we had preserved intact the commission's basic authority. But that ended the short list of consolations.

Senator Packwood's outrage served as a bittersweet reminder that only three years earlier we had confidently relied on just such spontaneous moral outrage to inhibit Congress from entanglement with the children's advertising proceeding. But the broadcast, cereal, and sugar industries had demonstrated a deft capacity to deflect such outrage in both the media and Congress, and it was they who had successfully seized or confused the symbols of debate.

Business had thus succeeded in neutralizing the unique political weapon that had made the entrepreneurial politics celebrated by James Q. Wilson possible: an unambiguous citizen outrage focused upon a consensual legislative remedy.

The outrage successfully fanned and focused in the sixties by Ralph Nader on the automobile companies' neglect of safe design and by Warren Magnuson on the cotton textile manufacturers' ne-

53. United Press International wire service report, April 24, 1980.

glect of child burnings, and channeled into the political energy behind the passage of remedial legislation, had dissipated.

In its place there existed a cacophony of conflicting claims on public outrage that succeeded in restoring Lindblom's stated condition for business's predominant influence in public decision making: citizen confusion and ambivalence.[54]

The FTC Improvements Act that emerged from the Congress was in all its provisions a businessman's relief act. It contained broadly speaking two categories of provisions: the first, primarily reflecting the Carter administration's own legislative proposals, could fairly be advertised as regulatory reform measures, such as assuring advance notice of contemplated rule making to affected businesses and the opportunity to educate agencies on the impact of contemplated remedies. Such provisions may well have been relatively benign, but they nonetheless evidence Congress's priority responsiveness to business, not consumer, concerns.

The second category of provisions could only be regarded as spurious regulatory reforms: naked political sorties by the affected industries to evade public accountability for commercial abuse and consumer injury.

This from the Congress that, for the prior decade, had consistently urged the commission to undertake these very same initiatives, and in general had flogged the commission for its attention to trivia and lack of responsiveness to serious consumer concerns.

As for the commission's last-minute reprieve, it should have been clear then, as it was to become later, that commission initiatives that theoretically survived because of press attention or presidential intervention would yet be stillborn—that for better or worse there is no such thing as an independent agency. The commission of the 1980s would reflect the implied as well as the express will of Congress, just as had the commission of the 1970s.

It was not therefore surprising that commission staff working on the children's rule-making proceeding subsequently concluded that though there was indeed substantial evidence of the deceptive nature of children's advertising, no feasible remedy could be devised and the proceeding should therefore be closed. The commission agreed.

Nor is it surprising that the commission has not yet requested authority from the Commerce Committee of either house to resume

54. Lindblom, *Politics and Markets*, pp. 210–11.

its insurance studies. Nor that the commission found that cigarette warnings in advertising were grossly inadequate and should be replaced by a series of rotating warnings, but hesitated to propose a rule requiring such warnings.[55] Nor that no new monopolization cases have been brought against any agricultural cooperative.

No longer were congressmen and senators fearful of being labeled "tools of the special interests" or anti-consumer. They had acquired a new arsenal of self-protective rhetoric, the rhetoric of indignation at the depravity of "over-zealous regulators"; of the undermining of productivity and of excessive cost burdens passed on to consumers; of regulatory overkill, and unelected bureaucrats tying the hands of American business in the fight to the competitive death against the Japanese industrial menace.

These epithets provided a respectable cover of rhetorical outrage for any congressman who chose to serve the interests of any industry, whether local or merely generously forthcoming with campaign financing. Whether justly provoked or spurious, business-stimulated congressional outrage was treated with equal respect and gravity by Congress and, in large part, by the media as well.

That there were indeed genuine and distressing flaws in various government regulatory programs—flaws that most assuredly had to be addressed through oversight and genuine regulatory reform—cannot obscure the fact that these fashionable epithets were grossly abused and manipulated by business lobbies, which sought nothing more patriotic than to be left alone, regardless of the merits of regulatory intervention.

The only controversial commission initiative that to this date has survived substantially intact is the funeral rule, and that can be attributed to the persistence of uniquely favorable conditions.

The rule itself is clear, simple, understandable to laymen, and involves the conservative proposition that the arrangers of funerals ought to supply basic price information. There is, moreover, a strong, articulate, politically awakening constituency among the elderly, as well as broad media and popular consensus on the rightness and fairness of the proposed rule—there was universal and unqualified media condemnation of the congressional effort to terminate the rule as lobby-inspired.

Opposition, on the other hand, comes from an industry that to be

55. See Federal Trade Commission, *Staff Report on the Cigarette Advertising Investigation* (Washington, D.C.: Government Printing Office, 1981).

sure has political access through its individual members, but never-theless consists of small businesses isolated from the main business community and relatively low in public standing and legitimacy. Not even the Chamber of Commerce undertook to support the fu-neral directors' cause.

Yet even the funeral rule still faces the likely prospect of congres-sional veto in the near future.

4

Consumer Strategies for the 1980s:
The Renewal of Consumer Outrage and Regulatory Legitimacy

Today in Washington, we liberals (who prefer for the moment to be known as progressives) ricochet between doomsday scenarios and portents of restoration. Liberal discourse abounds in wishful symbols, that of the pendulum being perhaps the most reassuring. Resisting the lessons of a deflated optimism, I do see the seeds of a resurgent consumer entrepreneurial politics replanted and sprouting in soil made fertile by the crude business sycophancy of the Reagan administration. As Joseph Kraft observes: "The president's Achilles' heel is a respect for private wealth so ingenuous as to promote inequities in public policy and sleaziness among government officials."[1]

Certainly, the public, though still bemused by Reagan's persona, increasingly perceives his administration as tilting precipitously toward wealth and privilege. I believe the images of ostentation struck so graphically at the Reagan inaugural celebrations are sharply etched in the recesses of the public mind. To be sure, so long as the majority of middle- and working-class Americans continue to hope that the Reagan economic policies will bring them economic succor, these images may remain dormant. But if those expectations are frustrated, if the "born-again" economy is stillborn (as it now appears to be), the images of corporate favoritism will center in the

1. Kraft, "Reagan's Nemesis Now . . ." *Washington Post*, July 19, 1981, p. C7.

119

public consciousness. Reagan may succeed where Nader fell short in rekindling public outrage.

There are other grounds for restrained optimism. Reagan's regulators are courteous and wear blue ties, with emblems neatly ranked in rows. They are otherwise distinguished mostly by their chronic myopia in overlooking consumer disadvantage and abuse at the hands of producers. As a minority commissioner, therefore, I foresee no dearth of opportunities for impassioned dissent. There are also murmurings and rumblings in Congress at the extent of this administration's indifference to corporate gigantism and consumer injury. Outside Congress, many consumer leaders have returned to consumer advocacy seasoned by experience and legitimized by the cachet of official tenure in the Carter administration.

After a period I. F. Stone uncharitably characterized as collaborationist, the press is restive. I take some comfort from the restiveness of investigative journalists nostalgic for Watergate, but undernourished by the relative integrity of the Ford and Carter administrations. The Reagan administration can seek to throttle the Freedom of Information Act and "sunshine" laws and disclaim any interest in corporate records or reports; but no secrets are safe where the Xerox machine lurks. The pages of the *Washington Post* have again begun to bristle with tales of government malfeasance and neglect, reflected in resurgent editorial outrage. And the continued popular appeal of "60 Minutes" and Bill Moyers suggests that the public appetite for revelations of corporate misdeeds is not sated.

As we have seen, too, the polls show both a firm underpinning of public support for the regulation of business and acute discomfort with perceived big business dominance of government decision making.

But the pendulum, should it swing back toward the populist or liberal pole, will still encounter drag from a Congress rooted more firmly than ever in its business constituency. Perhaps the ratchet is a more appropriate symbol than the pendulum. As we have seen, incremental progress has been achieved in consumer and environmental standards and restraints that do not threaten entrenched market strategies or profits. The image of the ratchet suggests that though such regulation will be loosened, the level of protection will not fall to preexisting levels.[2]

_____

2. For the metaphor of the ratchet, I am indebted to Robert Harris of the Graduate School of Business Administration at the University of California, Berkeley. See also

Ironically, many businessmen, confounding their supplicants in the Reagan administration, appear to accept the basic thrust of some new regulations as just, generally tolerable, and fairly responsive to public need and demand, though we can certainly anticipate continued allergic reaction by business to the cost burdens of regulation. Moreover, as we proceed into this new regulatory era, it will become increasingly difficult for business to fob off its poor economic performance, since the Reagan administration's loudly trumpeted regulatory relief is unlikely to produce a traceable resurgence in business productivity or vigor.

But as the image of the ratchet suggests, only part of past regulatory gains will be secured, indicating a porous consumer and environmental safety net. The equity and structural concerns from which Congress, the FTC, and others have retreated will remain politically untouchable in the face of immovable business resistance.

But if we assume a resurgence of political entrepreneurial leadership, press responsiveness, and rekindled public outrage at corporate abuse and government complicity in such abuse, we still confront the inherent limits to entrepreneurial politics—a politics that, as we have seen, rests upon the confluence of public rage and a clear and evident remedy possessed of universal legitimacy.

Before we prescribe or predict the course of consumer strategies for the 1980s, we need to draw from the previous chapters some measured conclusions on these inherent limits to entrepreneurial politics.

First, public outrage almost always erupts too late, binding commitments having been exacted by prudent lobbies long before the press and public are aroused by the drama of pending infamy. Once roused, public indignation is difficult to sustain, easily diverted, and capable at best of being focused on a particular legislative remedy only briefly, while the producer interest perseveres. Outrage over consumer issues is easily crowded off the national agenda.

Second, public outrage can be vented or deflated by a skillfully shaped token response—what Nader sardonically dismisses as a "no-law law." Thus, public concern over the unrestrained marketing of cigarettes to young people, especially through television advertising, was deflated by congressional passage in 1965 of a law

---

Eugene Bardach and Robert A. Kagan, *Going By the Book: The Problem of Regulatory Reasonableness* (Philadelphia: Temple University Press, 1982), ch. 7.

requiring that a mild warning be printed on cigarette packages, a requirement already scheduled to take effect through an FTC rule, without congressional action.[3] While appearing to have taken a bold step in mandating the package warning, Congress in the same act forbade either the Federal Trade Commission or any state or local government from requiring a warning or otherwise restricting cigarette advertising.

By 1969–70, public discomfort with broadcast advertising of cigarettes had again become acute. In the interim, the Federal Communications Commission, in part because its new chairman, a Mormon, shared the Mormon rejection of smoking, had imposed a rule requiring broadcasters to present anti-smoking counter-commercials at a rough ratio of one for each three cigarette ads. Pursuing a strategy of calculated withdrawal, the tobacco industry determined that it was in its own best interest to vanish from television. The anti-smoking commercials were potentially effective in undermining the cigarette market. Commercially, the intense, head-on competition through saturation television advertising in the marketing of essentially undifferentiated products had become increasingly expensive and inefficient. The companies calculated correctly that a withdrawal of advertising from television would not substantially undermine the existing market for cigarettes. Finally, by withdrawing from television, they would have removed from public consciousness the most visible goad and stimulus to government regulation: the ubiquitous presence in the home of the cigarette commercials.

Congress was pleased to oblige such corporate statesmanship. That the cigarette industry's strategy was sound can now be confirmed by its continued health and prosperity ten years later and by the absence from the public agenda of any serious threat of new regulatory action to curb cigarette advertising, despite the FTC's best efforts to the contrary. So when we reflect longingly on the "high consumerism" of the sixties, our nostalgia is freighted with the knowledge that during that very period, *no* government action

3. The Federal Cigarette Labeling and Advertising Act of 1965, (Pub. L. No. 89–92, 79 Stat. 283) required that all cigarette packages bear the warning: "Caution: Cigarette Smoking May Be Dangerous to Your Health." In 1970 Congress amended this warning to read: "Warning: The Surgeon General Has Determined That Cigarette Smoking Is Dangerous to Your Health" (15 U.S. Code § 1331 et seq. [1976]). For a more detailed discussion of the politics of cigarette labeling and advertising, see A. Lee Fritschler, *Smoking and Politics: Policymaking and the Federal Bureaucracy* (Englewood Cliffs, N.J.: Prentice-Hall, 1969).

was taken that seriously threatened the short-term market or profitability of the most lethal consumer product ever openly sold in this country. All it took was a little skillful corporate yin to deflect the yang of public outrage.

A third lesson is that entrepreneurial politics are also limited to mating patently matched cures with salient evils, such as flammability standards to cope with fabric flammability or auto-safety standards to mitigate the "second collision." Many of the most potentially significant consumer initiatives failed because the remedies were too complex or abstract or not readily obvious.

The proposed Consumer Protection Agency, which the American public favored by a majority of nearly two to one,[4] nevertheless suffered from an undertow of public disaffection with big government. The cause of generic consumer advocacy did not offer a manifest legal right or remedy for a specific consumer injury. The Consumer Protection Agency was manifestly more government; and what it would *do* was obscure.

The failure of the consumer agency legislation is often cited as a benchmark for the decline of Nader's political influence. Given the heroic business lobbying energies deployed against the agency bill and the inability of its proponents to draw upon focused public outrage, what is surprising is not that the legislation failed of passage, but that it came so close.

A similar fate befell Senator Magnuson's effort to enact consumer class action legislation, so that consumers damaged by common, but relatively small, product defects or other consumer injuries could band together in a common suit to obtain relief.[5] By enabling consumers to spread the otherwise inhibiting cost of attorneys among their fellow victims, the class action made self-help remedies feasible. But the concept again proved too abstract and remote for popular appeal. The very term "class action" conveyed nothing to most consumers. It was also a remedy unattached to a specific injury; "class actions" never resonated in the public breast.

"No-fault" auto insurance was another reform that fell by the way under the pressure of the trial lawyers, who saw their essential livelihood—the national market for arms and legs and whiplash injuries—potentially destroyed by an insurance system designed

4. See *Roper Reports*, no. 77–6 (New York: The Roper Organization, 1977), section G, question no. 17.
5. U.S., Congress, Senate, 92d Cong., 1st sess., 1971, S. 1222.

simply to compensate accident victims. The relationship between a tort-based automobile accident liability system and high automobile insurance rates proved too complex and remote to galvanize public support. Similarly, the benefits of federal chartering of major corporations, however theoretically sound, must have appeared abstract, complex and remote to a general public that has never doubted the legitimacy of the corporation.[6]

A fourth limitation: even where a critical mass of public outrage exists and is perceived by Congress as a demand for government intervention, certain potential remedies prove beyond the pale of public ideological limits. Regulation, yes. Competitive *public* enterprise, no.

Thus, at the height of the public outrage and antipathy toward the oil companies in the early 1970s, broad public support existed (and persists to this day) for price controls on oil and gas, the traditional regulatory response. But only about a third of the U.S. public were prepared to support the proposed Magnuson-Stevenson oil and gas regulatory reform legislation of 1974,[7] which would have created a federal oil and gas corporation to serve as a competitive goad and yardstick against which to measure the performance of energy companies in developing reserves on publicly owned lands.

One defeat Nader and Magnuson suffered, even at the crest of public support for auto-safety legislation, was in their effort to impose criminal as well as civil penalties for *knowing* and *willful* violations by corporate executives of automobile safety standards. Nader has characterized consumer initiatives as efforts to police "crime in the suites" and has evoked, in debate on auto safety and other product, workplace, and environmental safety issues, the image of "corporate violence." There is, of course, a difference between the immediacy of a mugging and slow death from exposure to a carcinogen; and the term violence connotes suddenness as well as injury. Yet the concept that knowing and deliberate exposure of another human to such a risk is a form of murder does not do violence to language.

But it doesn't sell. Senator Pastore, who led the successful Senate floor fight to delete the criminal penalty provisions from the auto-

6. For a detailed discussion of the federal chartering issue, see Mark Green, Ralph Nader, and Joel Seligman, *Taming the Giant Corporation* (New York: W. W. Norton and Co., 1976).
7. U.S. Congress, Senate, 93d Cong., 2d sess., 1974, S. 2506.

safety law, considered the very presence of those provisions a slander against corporate executives. Whether the public generally shared his revulsion is problematic. What is clear is that the public is disinclined to equate corporate behavior, no matter how deliberate or injurious, with street crime.

Fifth. In Washington, and especially in Congress, we have seen that public outrage is filtered and mediated by a structured environment calculated to dull and defuse outrage. Politically attuned Washington was appalled at Nader's "cruel insensitivity" in telling Senator Jake Garn of Utah, who had lost his wife in an automobile accident some three years earlier, that "some senator's personal tragedy might not have occurred if the auto industry had listened to us [on safety in automobile design] in the early years."[8]

Like other civilized Washingtonians, I too winced at this breach of "common decency" and privacy. Yet Nader was technically right. An air bag might well have saved the life of Garn's wife and the lives of other people—she and thousands of others now dead might be alive. His statement was not gratuitous, but a response to an at least equally intemperate attack by Senator Garn on the entire auto-safety program, in which he declared, "If the American consumers knew what you've cost us in the name of consumerism Mr. Nader, they'd run you out of the country."[9]

Nader was again seeking to break through the pious abstractions of regulatory reform to the underlying pain and suffering and life at stake. But Washington chose to perceive his response as a political rejoinder below the belt. He provoked outrage from Garn and other critics of regulation, who raged against his "cruelty." From those who were more sympathetic to Nader's objectives, he evoked at best discomfort at his breech of social convention.

Upon reflection, the incident teaches not Nader's insensitivity so much as the ease with which Congress in its social environment is deflected from focus and concern over the human costs of its actions or inactions. And it also illustrates the inherent limits to a politics that depends upon the continuous renewal of public outrage when public indifference or imperviousness forces consumer advocates to extreme rhetoric that may repel as much as inspire.

Nader's attacks on Senators Ford and Danforth in their home

8. "Nader, Garn Clash Bitterly," *Washington Post*, January 21, 1979.
9. Ibid.

states also pushed hard upon the acceptable limits of political discourse, yet were tactically essential to stimulate public awareness and concern about the role of these senators. The strategic demands for increasingly harsh and extreme rhetoric thus simultaneously tend to undermine the legitimacy of the advocate.

There is little doubt that the course of the FTC's children's advertising proceeding would have run somewhat more smoothly had I not spoken out on the issues as an advocate of constraints. The resulting image of the commission under my leadership as a consumer advocacy agency did tend to undermine the agency's legitimacy as a neutral fact-finding, quasi-judicial institution, thereby aggravating the commission's vulnerability to industry lobbying. Yet there was some validity to our assumption that, if children's advertising were to be placed on the public agenda, and the issues framed and elevated in public consciousness as a means of bolstering congressional resistance to lobbying attacks on the proceeding, there were few advocacy voices that had such ready access to the media as the chairman of the FTC.

Thus, the role of the regulator, the unelected bureaucrat, as a public advocate to counterbalance the advocacy resources of business is inherently limited by the conflicting need for the regulator to maintain his own legitimacy as impartial decision maker.

Finally, it is, or should be, evident by now that the notion of a regulatory agency independent of business political power (whether exercised directly through influential contact or indirectly through the White House or Congress) is illusory. The *progressive* vision reflected in Franklin D. Roosevelt's exultant imagery of the independent agency as a "tribune of the people" standing between the public and "private greed" was a romantic and *flawed* vision.[10]

THE SPROUTING OF THE GRASSROOTS

During my first years at the FTC, I adopted the habit of "riding circuit" every month or so to one of our ten regional offices. As a professed Democrat, I also made each of these visits the occasion for cultivating the FTC's grassroots. Whether it was Cleveland, Denver, or Chicago, we would arrange a day of meetings with representa-

---

10. Quoted in "Congressional Democratic Policy Statement on Regulatory Reform," paper presented to the White House, mimeographed, June 25, 1975.

tives of consumer and small business groups. It probably demeans these sessions unnecessarily to view them as bureaucratic noblesse oblige, but they were a pale form of public participation.

These meetings were invariably both satisfying and marred. They were satisfying because they confirmed that we were working on many of the right things: complaints of credit discrimination, new housing defects, auto-repair fraud, unsatisfied warranty complaints. To many of the consumer issues they raised, we were indeed attempting to respond. The meetings were marred, however, because many of the problems that evoked the most pain were generally beyond our reach, such as ruinous rents and utility rates. These "hard-core" issues were beyond our effective control. I came away feeling that we were responsive to *real* concerns, but that we rarely dealt with *central* concerns.

There was also an understandable passivity in the relationship of these citizens to their federal government. They confirmed our choice of investigative regulatory targets. They were for the most part grateful that a federal agency had time to spare for them, and they seemed to be generally satisfied with our efforts, which, however removed from their central concerns, were nevertheless directed at ameliorating their lives, rather than burdening them. They were respectful, sometimes skeptical, only rarely insistent. Like the relationship between the consumer entrepreneurs of the sixties and the public, the leadership of these groups was supportive of our efforts, but they were essentially passive recipients of federal largess.

There were, however, exceptions.

As I was completing one such visit to the commission's Denver regional office, preparing to move on to Los Angeles, I received an unsettling call from my office in Washington. Consumer and citizen groups in the Los Angeles area had been dutifully contacted and invited to meet with the chairman of the FTC, and plans for that meeting were proceeding. But there was one group, UNO, the United Neighborhood Organizations, a group representing the Hispanic people of East Los Angeles, who were not at all gracious about the invitation. They insisted that they had in vain been demanding an appointment with me for the past year to discuss a matter of grave concern to their members (that we had no record of their request was of little interest to them.) UNO was not content to be part of a generalized, token meeting with disparate groups. Unless I agreed to meet with a representative committee of UNO, they would picket the commission's Los Angeles office while I was there. They were not prepared to disclose the nature of their grievance; it would wait for the meeting.

As Ralph Nader has argued, to be democratically accountable, institutional power, in a democracy, must be insecure. I was insecure. Who were these people and what did they want of me? The one thing I knew was that I did not care to be picketed. I took the only rational course open. I agreed to meet with them.

It turned out that they had a problem we really couldn't do much about, or at least we ordinarily *wouldn't* have done anything about. But this group of citizens armed with the energy born of indignation was not to be easily satisfied. The committee, led by Father Olivares, included a trained community organizer and several members of the elected leadership of UNO. The organization had experienced explosive growth in the past several years, drawing upon the organizational strength and legitimacy of local churches, until it had grown to include hundreds of thousands of East Los Angeles Hispanics. More to the immediate point, it was capable of assembling 5,000 or more members, if necessary, to confront an unresponsive bureaucrat.

The issue was red-lining discrimination by auto-insurance companies against the Hispanics and blacks of East Los Angeles. Simply put, the auto insurance rates in East Los Angeles were close to double those of adjacent Beverly Hills, though accident and loss data, they insisted, justified no such discrimination.

They had come to me and the Federal Trade Commission because they feared that the state insurance commissioner, whom they had been vigorously petitioning, would not respond unless he sensed the potential threat of federal intervention and pressure. They wanted the commission to investigate the discrimination and to do so publicly and ostentatiously so as to put pressure on the state. They did not know or care that the FTC had no direct jurisdiction over insurance rates. They did know that it had responsibility under the Equal Credit Opportunity Act for policing credit discrimination. [11]

I could have said, "There is nothing we can do under our law." Perhaps they would have gone away without picketing. But I didn't do that. Here, for the first time in my experience as chairman, were people who had come directly to us as a community out of anger and

11. Equal Credit Opportunity Act, 15 *U.S. Code* § 1691 et seq. (1976).

frustration at the unresponsiveness of both insurance companies and state officials. So much of what we did, while it could be of great economic benefit to consumers, seemed remote and abstract. But here were people confronting injustice, demanding our help.

I told Father Olivares and his colleagues that they must understand that there was no possibility that the commission could directly affect auto-insurance rates in East Los Angeles; but that I would make a bargain with them. I would agree to meet with their representatives formally and publicly (with the Washington representatives of Los Angeles media present) to hear the grievances of UNO against both insurance companies and the California Insurance Commissioner. And we would undertake, broadly construing our powers under the Equal Credit Opportunity Act, an investigation of auto insurance and related credit discrimination in East Los Angeles. They must know, however, that a report was all they would get, because we were unlikely to find violations of the specific laws we enforced. If they believed that the meeting and the promise of the report would give them the leverage they needed in California, we would do it. They agreed; the meeting was held; the commission announced its investigation. *Three weeks later Allstate announced that it was dropping its auto-insurance rates* in East Los Angeles by a third. Others followed. I do not know whether we made the difference, but I like to think so.

Why does this incident stand out? On reflection, I think I was drawn into this venture partly out of fear—the fear of picketing, of confrontation with 5,000 massed, angry citizens—but also partly out of respect for a community and its leaders who were prepared to demand and fight for their rights. And, finally, I was intrigued by the opportunity, with a relatively small exercise of commission energy, to make a difference in the lives of people who had not gotten much from life or their government. The incident also stands out because *we* were not the entrepreneurs. We were one of the instruments available to citizens acting on their own behalf. We were responsive; but we were not the initiators.

There was comfort, too, in the thought that the easily anticipated letter of indignation from a California congressman berating the commission for treading on the jurisdictional toes of the California Insurance Commissioner would be met with a polite, unassertive response from the commission—and a local congressional office surrounded by pickets from UNO. In the event, we received no such letters.

I remember UNO and I remember the militant members of the American Association of Retired Persons who angrily confronted many of those congressmen who had voted insouciantly for the Russo amendment to kill the commission's funeral rule. The elderly were angry. Their anger was organized and focused through an organization that had begun as little more than a front for a life insurance company and had been transformed by its members into a grassroots economic union, increasingly militant in demanding government response to the economic concerns of the elderly, among which, unsentimentally, were the high prices and over-reaching sales tactics of too many funeral vendors.

I thought of UNO and I thought of AARP and the National Council of Senior Citizens as I sat among the participants in the September 1981 "Taking Charge" Conference in Washington, held to honor the tenth anniversary of Ralph Nader's Public Citizen and the public interest research groups (PIRGs). It was, of course, a sentimental reunion. We were the Old Guard. We had old victories and fresh defeats to retell and share.

There were two sides of Nader's public role represented there. We were the veterans of the Washington campaigns—Wilson's political entrepreneurs. Labels are wisely skirted, especially these days, but it might be said that we represented the late New Deal liberal tradition. If neo-conservatives such as Irving Kristol had hit any targets in their condemnation of liberal elites, they had struck at least glancing blows off all of us.[12] We were disproportionately Ivy Leaguers, do-gooders, knee-jerk liberals, occupied with alleviating the hardship of others, fueled by faith in the capacity of government to represent the people against "private greed," so long as the government was peopled or stimulated by us. We defended ourselves against charges of elitism with the strong evidence that the principles we stood for and the causes we enlisted in enjoyed popular, if sometimes passive, support. But if we were "for the people," for the most part we were not comfortably "of the people."

But the Nader conference, entitled "Taking Charge: The Next Ten Years," was not *our* conference. It represented instead the flowering of what had always been a second side to Nader's leadership—the populist, as contrasted with the liberal. This was the Nader who

12. See Irving Kristol, *Two Cheers for Capitalism* (New York: Basic Books, 1978); for more on the neoconservative case against the "new class" see B. Bruce Briggs, ed., *The New Class* (New Brunswick, N.J.: Transaction Books, 1979).

spoke not so much of safety air bags as of "many outlets of citizen involvement and responsibility," of "new citizen energies."

This was the Nader of the PIRG's preoccupied with the mechanisms of grassroots organization and involvement. This was the Nader who, while calling upon government to carry out its responsibilities to all citizens, shared the populist distrust of government. For many businessmen, Nader is the great regulator, the symbol of massive government regulation. Yet Nader's popular appeal was built upon his attacks on unresponsive government bureaucracy as well as on business.

In seeking to structure regulatory schemes, he had always pressed for new forms of direct participation, such as rights of petition, bureaucratic accountability to citizens' action, or self-help remedies like consumer class actions, which bypass bureaucracies. Even Nader's blueprint for corporate accountability, embodied in the concept of federal chartering, was designed not to impose new levels of government supervision, but to constitutionalize rights empowering affected consumers, workers, and communities to take direct action in the courts to hold corporations accountable. Nader viewed the law as embodying the power of government to restrain corporate abuse; simultaneously, he saw the need to make government power equally accountable to direct citizens' action. Nader considers the initiative and referendum the truly great and lasting heritage of the progressive movement.

Before the first summer vacation I took after becoming chairman of the commission, I had asked several friends and colleagues for recommended readings. Nader's first choice was *Democratic Promise* by Lawrence Goodwyn, the history of the populist movement of the late nineteenth century in the South, Midwest, and Southwest.[13] Goodwyn helped me to understand why, in the late 1970s, Nader had placed a very high priority on legislation to create a national cooperative bank to provide technical assistance and seed money for consumer cooperatives.

Democratic Promise gave historic confirmation to the Nader conviction that organized citizens' participation in democratic self-governance was possible. The populist movement, as depicted by Goodwyn, grew organically out of the desperate efforts of farmers

13. Goodwyn, *Democratic Promise: The Populist Movement in America* (New York: Oxford University Press, 1976).

to band together collectively in the farmers' alliances—buying and selling cooperatives that formed a last defense against exploitation by banks, seed and implement sellers, and grain merchants. Out of the cooperative experience grew a sense of community and shared purpose, which blossomed into a political movement. And I was not surprised to find that Lawrence Goodwyn was a principal speaker at the "Taking Charge" conference's plenary session on "developing the tools of democratic organization."

There was little mention, if any, at the Nader conference of the lost consumer protection agency to which many of us, most of all Nader himself, had devoted energy and emotional investment for those ten years. There was scant mention of the safety air bag, the specific regulatory issue that, more than any other, had drawn Nader's deep emotional involvement. Indeed, the traditional consumer issues were only touched on in passing, as the conference focused on economic issues that were both broader and narrower than the legislative and regulatory issues we had worked on. Broader issues were raised in speeches that decried the massive impact of the government's macroeconomic policies entrenching wealth and privilege and undermining the broad gains of two decades of political struggle to shape a government more nearly responsive to the rights and needs of the vast majority than to those of the privileged.

Down-to-earth organizing tactics were the thrust of those speakers and participants who represented the populist organizers. They emphasized the energy and potential strength that lay in organizing around salient community issues: utility rates, rents, tax equity, toxic contamination of communities, the building of co-ops, and work-place democracy.

Perhaps the Nader conference symbolized the transition of consumerism from a liberal to a populist movement, a transition ironically reflecting the evident attitudes of citizens far more faithfully than the Reagan administration's perceived conservatism. For those very polls that demonstrate continued public demand for government intervention against business abuse also express a strong preference for regulations empowering citizens—regulations that give consumers more information with which to bargain on their own behalf, greater rights and self-help remedies. A recent Harris poll on attitudes towards regulation concluded: "Americans do not believe that industry will reform itself. But at the same time, they do not see big government as their savior either. Indeed, they want an opening

up of the bargaining and regulatory process to allow citizen participation on a scale never before witnessed in human history."[14]

CONCLUSION

In Charles E. Lindblom's opinion, business tends to deflect regulatory thrusts, no matter how well intentioned, to its own ends,
through its primacy in our economic and political system. In the
1960s and early 1970s that harsh judgment appeared to be leavened
by consumerism, environmentalism, and other public-interest successes, but today we find Lindblom's belief shared by populists and
conservatives alike. Wall Street conservative William Simon observes that

> the dynamics of the political system favor groups that are concen-
> trated and actively involved in the regulatory process, with high
> stakes in the outcome of some specific bureaucratic decision. Such
> people consistently prevail over those who are dispersed and far from
> the regulatory system, with a small stake in any given decision (al-
> though a big stake in the overall process)—in other words, American
> consumers.

Translated into song, his views are indistinguishable from the
campaign theme of Jim Hightower, a Texas populist who first spent
time as a staff member for Senator Fred Harris, then founded the
Washington-based Agribusiness Accountability Project, wrote two
books,[15] and served as Fred Harris's campaign manager in the 1976
presidential campaign. Hightower then returned to Texas to run as
an "economic populist" for the Texas Railroad Commission, the
superutility that controls the economic lifeblood of Texas. In 1973 he
won 48 percent of the vote against a candidate heavily funded by
energy and utility industries. His theme song:

> Them that's got is them that gets
> And I ain't got nothing yet.[16]

14. Cited in Lawrence Goodwyn, "A Democratic Revival," *New Republic*, March 14,
1981, p. 36.
15. *Eat Your Heart Out: How Food Profiteers Victimize the Consumer* (New York: Random House, 1976) and *Hard Tomatoes, Hard Times: The Hightower Report* (New York:
Hippocrene Books, 1978).
16. "An Interview with Jim Hightower," *Working Papers*, July–August 1981, p. 51.

Hightower tells of giving a speech in Nebraska while he was operating out of Washington, running the Agribusiness Accountability Project. Talking to farmers about "corporate agribusiness eating up the farmer and consumers alike," he tells of a farmer who rushed up to him sputtering, "You're right; that's absolutely right, what are we going to do about it?" And Hightower explained how they had to persuade the Federal Trade Commission to bring an antitrust action against the food conglomerates. "No," said the man, "I mean now. I'm losing my farm this year; what are we going to do now?"[17] Hightower concludes,

> We have to go out and deal with him at his level, which is the only level that counts. It's the only level that counts because it's the only level where there is real pain. But it's the only level where there are real solutions. That's where the power comes from, and we've been fooling ourselves about power. Basically we shouldn't be allowed to. I don't want anybody using my power.[18]

Simon says forget the government; trust the market. Hightower says forget Washington—for a while—and trust the people to help themselves.

I know, too, that whatever the sins and overreaching of the business lobbies, the Chamber of Commerce had organized real people. However artificially stimulated and misled, their outrage and energy were palpable. Their grassroots may have underlain lawns of privilege, but they were rooted in communities and they were real. And, at least before the elderly began to respond to the congressional attack on the funeral rule, most congressmen could say in earnest, "I never heard a word from a constituent supporting the Federal Trade Commission."

I do not believe that consumer issues will ever be central to the political debate in this country, but many consumer issues embody or symbolize key economic concerns, which can be part of an organizing effort. They symbolize the imbalance of economic and political power, and they are, for the most part, unifying issues among disparate groups. Only a used car dealer would not be pleased to have effective restrictions on fraud and misrepresentation in the sale of used cars; only the funeral directors would protest the requirement that they tell the truth and provide the bereaved with a little

17. Ibid., p. 52.
18. Ibid.

more information. Unlike social issues, consumer issues tend not to be broadly divisive.

I don't know whether "grassroots democracy" or "the new populism" or "the backyard revolution," as Harry Boyte calls it, can work.[19] I know that the populist movement in the nineteenth century flamed briefly, until its heat was drawn off by racist Democrats. There is nothing in my experience that tells me directly whether a grassroots political movement, part of which is made up of the consumer agenda, can be built within the Democratic party out of the pain of economic abuse and disadvantage.

Still, I cite no less an authority than Wilson Wyatt, Jr., manager of corporate affairs and communications for Brown & Williamson, who testified with great force and vehemence, perhaps inadvertently, to the potential for grassroots democracy in this country. Speaking of the growing number of state and local referendums in recent years, Wyatt said: "The corporate interest . . . is not necessarily protected or advanced at the ballot box of popular sentiment . . . the loss of a single initiative can be devastating to the corporate interest." He protested that Proposition 5 on the 1978 California ballot, which was designed to expand non-smoking areas in public places, "cost $6.5 million to defeat." Wyatt concluded that "direct democracy becomes a threatening ballot box tool."[20]

If direct democracy can at least raise the costs of corrupting government decision making, then perhaps we could use a little more democracy.

19. Harry C. Boyte, *The Backyard Revolution: Understanding the New Citizen Movement* (Philadelphia: Temple University Press, 1981).

20. Wilson W. Wyatt, Jr., "The Voting Booth: Continuing Battleground for Corporations," Speech before the Public Affairs Council State Relations conference, July 7, 1980.

5

Lessons in Consumer Regulation:
Learned and Unlearned

I have been generous in allocating blame for consumer hard times to others. At the FTC, I have been especially forthcoming in acknowledging the errors of my predecessors.

Did we not, as David Vogel has argued, bring much of our misery upon ourselves by embracing intrusive, meddlesome, inefficient, overreaching, centralized, bureaucratic regulation?[1] And did we not thereby debase the public currency of all regulation?

No. And yes. I have argued strenuously in these pages that the consumer movement was laid low primarily by the reaction and revolt of business—though business was able to exploit the diffuse public disaffection with government and regulation to legitimize the dismantling of consumer and other regulations that have retained undiminished popular support.

But there were lessons we learned, sometimes painfully, in the course of transforming the consumer impulses of the sixties into the mature consumer regulation of the seventies. There were also lessons we refuse to learn.

We *have* learned greater respect for somber, unsentimental analysis of the effects of regulation. We, and here I believe I speak for many who view themselves as consumer advocates, have *not* learned to accept that the injustice and inequity arising from in-

1. See Vogel, "The Inadequacy of Contemporary Opposition to Business," *Dædalus*, Summer 1980, p. 109.

137

equality of bargaining power must be excluded from public policy if they cannot be measured in the economists' models.

We have learned to pay greater heed to the social value of the entrepreneur, to value market incentives as a creative force for productivity and growth. But we will not learn to tolerate the force with which those very incentives sweep aside the moral and ethical constraints that mark a civilized society.

We have learned that we must be accountable for the costs and burdens of regulation. But we will not concede that the economist's useful, but imperfect, tool of cost-benefit analysis dictates policy judgments on what is right and what is just.

We have been taught respect for a fallible bureaucracy's limitations in shaping human behavior. But we will not abandon faith in the role of government in a democratic society to redress inequity and to give appropriate expression to those non-market values people hold deeply.

Among the faiths that had not yet been shaken in the 1960s were faith in the efficacy of regulation, so long as the will and integrity of the legislator and the regulator were uncorrupted, and a counterpart faith in the capacity of American business to respond innovatively to regulatory commands by absorbing or dissipating the costs—a faith shared, at least implicitly, by business and consumer advocates alike.

When Detroit warned in the early 1960s that the mandatory installation of seat belts would cost more than consumers were willing to bear, then subsequently priced them around $10 per vehicle,[2] its apparent hypocrisy reinforced our skepticism, steeling our hearts even more against pleas of the hardships of regulation. Our awe for the herculean cost-absorptive powers of U.S. enterprise was simultaneously enhanced. Today, the skepticism remains; the awe has long since dissipated.

We boasted then, "There is a law that makes cars safer!" We know now, in a newly miserly universe, that in regulatory enterprise, as in so much else, there is no such thing as a free lunch. And laws don't make anything.

Many of the consumer laws enacted in the 1960s consisted essentially of the legislative naming of wrongs to be righted. To the regulators were left the remedies. Soon, we began hearing from the

---

2. See Ralph Nader, *Unsafe at Any Speed: The Designed-in Dangers of the American Automobile* (New York: Grossman, 1965), pp. 121, 128.

economists. We recoiled from economic models that reduced pain and suffering to numbers, milking "market failures" of their humanity. We were suspicious of elaborate analyses, invariably funded by business interests, that predictably and ritualistically challenged the efficacy of the regulatory remedies we had painstakingly constructed. Out of mingled distrust and frustration, consumer advocates denounced the economists and their misbegotten offspring, cost-benefit analysis.

I was a cost-benefit draft resister. Even when the more general benefits of economic analysis were sung, my guard was up. But at the FTC, with each proposed rule or case, I was confronted with the analysis of the commission's able economists, as well as its lawyers. The economists earned my grudging respect, not so much for their prescriptive counsel, which could be every bit as unworkable, even mad, as some of the lawyers' schemes, as for their dogged insistence that we *think through* the reality of what we believed we were achieving with our intervention in the marketplace.

Economists are very good indeed at framing questions that lawyers and consumer advocates have not asked. (Though the economists don't very much like having to deal with the sweaty, humanly imperfect answers to those questions.) They ask, "What do you think you are accomplishing with this rule? Who will benefit, who will pay? What else will happen as a result of this rule; who among competitors will be the winners and who the losers? In curing this marketplace failure, what others may you inadvertently cause, and what healthy market signals will you distort? Is there a less intrusive, less costly way to remedy the problem?"

And they ask that question most dreaded of all by the entrepreneurial regulator: "How secure are you that the world will be a better place for your intervention than if left alone?"

The economists helped teach us respect, if not reverence, for the marketplace—or, more precisely, for the power of market incentives, of self-interest. They have taught us how much more likely we are to gain our objectives by channeling the flow of such incentives than by vain efforts to block their passage.

We have learned from them that even where the impulse to regulate springs from deep wells of resentment at corporate abuse or neglect, we can end up punishing not just the miscreants, but their victims, the consumers, upon whom the costs of regulatory compliance are most often loaded.

So the central lesson is, simply, regulatory humility. This does not mean unblinking reverence for unregulated markets. It does mean acknowledging the need for enhanced understanding of the structure and dynamics of markets and of the cause, or causes, of market failure.

To recognize the value of cost-benefit analysis is not to surrender policy judgment to it. Its value lies in informing decision makers and the public of the dollars-and-cents consequences of alternative regulatory decisions. But it does not follow that we must be indentured as policy makers to the bottom line. We must not abandon our capacity to judge.

The numbers themselves are slippery in this kind of calculation. Costs are almost always more readily quantifiable than benefits. But even with the most sensitively calculated cost-benefit equation, a democratic society may give more weight to other shared values than to economic efficiency.

Take product safety, for example. As citizens, and as participants in the democratic political process, we may express our support for regulatory policies that give expression to our reverence for life itself, knowing when we do so that these decisions will not be without cost. We may do this even though, as individual buyers in the actual heat and pressure of purchasing decisions, we may well trade off safety for price. Why should we value our decisions as buyers over our decisions as citizens?

A recent, careful poll by the Opinion Research Corporation mocks the prevailing Washington wisdom that the public no longer supports consumer regulation. Perhaps most intriguing, that poll demonstrates that a substantial majority of the public understands full well that product safety standards add to the cost of consumer products. Even among those so informed, a substantial majority supports continued government regulation of minimum safe performance standards for consumer products.[3] (Of course, casual ex-

---

3. The report accompanying the poll states: "Focusing specifically on the government's regulations to insure the safety and dependability of consumer products or services, two-thirds of the public think that such regulations add at least a fair amount to the costs of the goods people buy. . . . Although more people now think that product safety and dependability requirements add significantly to costs, the majority of most segments of society still believe that these expenditures are worth it. Fewer than one-third of the people in any population sub-group feel that the costs are *not* merited. . . . Furthermore, almost two-thirds of the public believe it is necessary to pursue high standards for the protection of consumer interests regardless of the costs involved." (*ORC Public Opinion Index: Reports to Management*, vol. 39, nos. 1 and 2 [Princeton, N.J.: Opinion Research Corporation, January 1981], pp. 6–8.)

pressions of desire in shallow polls ought not to be lightly accepted as informed willingness to bear the costs of regulation.)

I retain ample reservations about cost-benefit methodology, but the *questions* it asks are nonetheless appropriate. This is especially true for an agency such as the FTC, whose primary mission is to improve the *economic* performance of the marketplace, rather than to shield the public from health or environmental effects on society, which are far more difficult to price. Let me suggest some of the questions the prudent regulator should ask, and what he or she might do with the answers:

1. *Is the rule consonant with market incentives to the maximum extent feasible?*

Respect for the power of self-interest—of market incentives—is surely one of the salient substantive lessons learned by consumer advocates in the past two decades.

Let me illustrate by recounting the commission's intellectual odyssey in pursuit of the optimum model state generic drug substitution law. The "anti-substitution" laws passed by most states at the behest of the pharmaceutical manufacturers prohibited the pharmacist from substituting an equivalent generic drug for the familiar brand name prescribed by the physician. We concluded that such laws were unduly restrictive and anti-competitive, a classic case of overregulation. We developed and urged state enactment of a model generic drug substitution law that permitted the pharmacist to substitute a generic equivalent drug, approved for safety and efficacy by the Food and Drug Administration, for a brand-name drug prescribed, unless the physician had expressly indicated that no substitution was desired.

Many consumer advocates, while supporting our efforts to reform state anti-substitution regulation, preferred an alternative form of generic drug regulation: mandatory sale of the least expensive generic substitute available and *mandatory* passing on of the full savings to the consumer, which they did not trust the pharmacist to do. As it turned out, they were right. Depending upon the availability of generic substitutes, the pharmacist would pass on the savings *only* to the extent that competition kept generic drug prices down. In the rough and tumble of the real marketplace, it turns out that only 50 to 90 percent of the savings were actually passed on to consumers under the model law. But we also know, because experience and theory combine to tell us so, that mandatory passing on of savings removes any incentive for pharmacists to stock generic substitutes, or encourages them to evade the law. We know, too, that no state attorney general has the will or resources to police all drug sales.

The model law, relying on competition and market incentives in a less than perfect marketplace, is less than perfect, but it does furnish consumers with substantial benefits, while a mandatory scheme, theoretically designed to assure a 100 percent benefit to consumers, does not work at all.

Respect for market incentives also led us at the FTC to strip away many of the elaborate cautionary disclosures to prospective students proposed in our vocational-schools rule.[4] Instead, we placed primary reliance upon a requirement that schools provide a pro rata refund for those students who did not complete the course (a provision already adopted voluntarily by some of the most reputable schools). This simple requirement redirected the schools' incentives to reflect the true worth of the course. So long as the student has to pay for the full course, no matter how ill-suited the student or how inadequate the course, the school has no incentive to screen students or improve its teaching. But the pro rata refund policy stimulates schools to do both.

In another example, the economists helped convince the commission to set a high priority on removing restrictions on competition within the professions self-imposed by professional societies in the name of ethics. Heeding their counsel, the commission lifted price advertising restraints on optometrists and opticians, freeing incentives for price competition. The benefits to the consumer were direct and dramatic; the price gap between jurisdictions in which restrictions on price advertising were allowed and those in which eyeglasses were freely advertised ranged between 25 and 40 percent.

2. *Will the remedy work?*

In the sixties there were certain goals we pursued because they intuitively seemed self-evidently right. Among them, for example, was the so-called cooling-off rule that we promulgated at the FTC.[5] This gave the consumer in a door-to-door sales transaction the right to change his or her mind and revoke the contract when no longer in

4. Proprietary Vocational and Home Study Schools Trade Regulation Rule 16 C.F.R. § 438 (1981).

5. Cooling-off Period for Door-to-Door Sales Trade Regulation Rule 16 C.F.R § 429 (1981), promulgated October 26, 1972.

the presence of a sometimes coercive or intimidating salesperson in the home. Three years after the effective date of the rule, we were confronted with evidence in the form of surveys that seemed to indicate that consumers rarely exercised the right. Of course, it was possible that the existence of the cooling-off provision had rid the marketplace of coercive selling techniques, but forty years of commission experience with direct selling abuses suggest that so felicitous an explanation was hardly likely. More likely, it appears that the language adopted by the commission was so obtuse and obscure that too few consumers understood their rights.

Similarly, in policing deceptive advertising, the commission's prized remedy of corrective advertising, which imposed upon the advertiser the affirmative obligation to include prescribed corrections in current ads to make up for past deception, also proved an elusive victory. As in the old tale of the indomitable elixir peddler proclaiming triumphantly that his product was guaranteed "100 percent adulterated," the ability of the advertiser to take a prescribed set of words and structure their effect is formidable. This is why the commission began to explore the possibility of handling such cases of past deception by imposing a "performance standard" on the corrective advertisement. That is, instead of imposing a specific warning produced by a committee of economists and lawyers, the commission would require that consumer misunderstanding caused by a misleading ad be cured by whatever means the advertiser chose, so long as the effect of the corrective ad campaign were to dissipate the misinformation within a prescribed period of time, as measured by the industry's own marketing survey techniques. This is but a logical extension of the principle that a goal-oriented performance standard, whether it be the reduction of pollution or safe performance (i.e., as prescribed in the original and farsighted auto-safety law of 1966)[6] will usually prove more effective than a detailed design standard, which, besides being less effective, can also have a chilling effect on technology. We know, too, that performance standards not only work, but provide incentives and create space for entrepreneurial responses that may not only achieve the desired goal, but enhance efficiency and productivity.

Just as performance standards can stimulate innovation, clumsy design standards or other proscriptive rules can inhibit it. Again, in most cases the effectiveness of a remedy will increase in direct pro-

6. Automobile Safety Act of 1966, Pub. L. No. 89–563, 80 Stat. 718.

portion to the extent to which it seeks to utilize market incentives rather than stifle them—unless the rule-making agency is prepared to deploy sufficient policing forces or employ rules that contain effective self-help remedies for the victims of the proscribed practices. This is especially true for decentralized industries and those made up of many small units.

3. *Will the chosen remedy minimize the cost burdens of compliance, consistent with achieving the objective?*

Whether it took "stagflation," the revitalization of business political action, the regulatory reform movement, or the loss of our own primitive faith in the miraculous innovative capacity of American business to convince us, let there be no doubt that the regulatory calculus must seek to minimize not only paperwork burdens but, more important, regulatory impediments to innovation, flexibility, and productivity.

In shaping its final funeral-price disclosure rule, the commission stripped its proposed record-keeping requirements to the bare minimum, requiring only the maintenance of records already kept as standard practice within the industry. There are, of course, trade-offs; record-keeping requirements are often essential to determine whether a violation of the law has occurred, and the elimination of such requirements increases the burden on the enforcement agency to trace the practices and prove violations. But, at least until the mid-seventies, there was a tendency to weight the balance in favor of enforcement, relatively heedless of the burdens.

A complicating aspect of burden analyses, but a crucial inquiry, relates to the cumulative burdens of remedies flowing from different regulatory authorities. The Regulatory Council, established during the Carter administration, was an important mechanism for facilitating efforts by regulators not only to avoid conflicting requirements, but also to consolidate and rationalize record keeping and reporting requirements. The Paperwork Reduction Act was a congressional trump card to top the Regulatory Council by vesting control over reporting requirements in the Office of Management and Budget.[7] OMB was given this authority despite the previous congressional mandate to the General Accounting Office to review all questionnaires for duplication.[8] To the extent that OMB supervision of paperwork burdens becomes yet another lever for business

7. Paperwork Reduction Act of 1980, Pub. L. No. 96–511, 94 Stat. 2812.
8. Federal Reports Act, 44 *U.S. Code* 3301.

to avoid appropriate scrutiny, the Paperwork Reduction Act will take its place in the ranks of regulatory reform overkills, but its articulated objectives are nonetheless valid.

4. *Will the benefits flowing from the rule to consumers or to competition substantially exceed the costs?*

In 1969 the Federal Trade Commission, then under the chairmanship of Caspar Weinberger, issued its long-awaited report on automobile quality control and warranty performance.[9] The industry record was dismal, the commission concluded. The country, urged the Weinberger FTC, faced no alternative but to treat the automobile industry as a public utility, following the models of the rail, trucking and aviation industries, regulated in the public interest by the Interstate Commerce Commission and Civil Aeronautics Board. A new automobile regulatory law must be enacted and a new automobile regulatory agency created to set minimum quality performance standards for automobiles, to fulfill such consumer desires as "lemon protection" (the mandatory replacement of the stubbornly defective new car) and to require that loan cars be supplied while cars under warranty were in the shop for repair.

As a Senate Commerce Committee staff member working for consumer advocate Senator Warren Magnuson, I was delighted with the study and felt it demonstrated a genuine commitment to the consumer by Chairman Weinberger. Perhaps, in retrospect, such a regulatory scheme *might* have stimulated a more competitive domestic automobile industry by the year 1981. But I doubt that Caspar Weinberger would today claim his early intellectual offspring, born in that era of high consumerism. A fundamental problem with that report was that nowhere in its pages does one find so much as a discussion of the costs of providing such protection, or of the tradeoffs between such costs and benefits to consumers. Such omissions are not likely to recur when we again see an administration responsive to the needs and concerns of consumers.

One issue popular among consumer advocates—popular, in fairness, because it evokes broad grassroots support—is the effort to maintain individual price marking of supermarket items and to resist replacement of such markings by shelf markings and computer printouts. That cause has always left me insecure, because I know of no evidence to suggest that individual price marking will benefit

9. U.S., Federal Trade Commission, "Report on Automobile Warranties" (1970).

consumers sufficiently to offset the costs (which, of course, are passed on) of the labor-intensive price-marking process.

Another example of dubious consumer benefit is the current rule, enforced by the FTC under congressional mandate,[10] that sellers furnish presale warranty information to prospective purchasers in a prescribed format.[11] "Presale availability" of warranty information is sound in principle, but the commission's studies demonstrate that few consumers have taken advantage of the information in the form in which it has been provided, while the requirement has imposed substantial costs on retailers. We have at minimum an obligation to consider a less burdensome, but still effective, means for assuring that those consumers who do desire to see and compare warranty information before purchase will be able to do so. To that end, the commission is considering changes in the presale availability rule.

Again, however, I would enter a caveat. Even in policing the marketplace for economic injury, as opposed to health or environmental injury, a rigid cost-benefit analysis may not be determinative. Values that cannot be reduced to dollars and cents must be considered in policing selling practices. For example, the desire to avoid the intimidation or coercion in their homes by door-to-door salesmen of the elderly, the uneducated poor, or non-English speaking immigrants is a value not easily quantifiable. Even the commission's traditional role in ensuring truth in the marketplace cannot easily be reduced to a cost-benefit formula, since both consumers and sellers have an overriding interest in preserving the integrity—and consumer *perception* of the integrity—of the marketing system. But who could place a dollar figure on "integrity"? It is perhaps for this reason that the advertising community has come to embrace the commission's advertising substantiation requirements, notwithstanding that the Reagan deregulators complain of its burdens.

5. *Will the rule or remedy adversely affect competition?*

The economists can surely take deserved credit for alerting us to the anti-competitive dangers in direct regulation of rates or entry into a marketplace. To their alarms can be traced much of the progress made in recent years toward eliminating such regulatory burdens on competition. But we also need be alert to the potentially

10. Consumer Product Warranties, Rules Governing Content of Warranties, 15 U.S. *Code* § 2302 (1976).

11. Pre-Sale Availability of Written Warranty Terms, 16 C.F.R. § 702 (1981).

discriminatory impact upon small competitors of consumer regulations entailing substantial compliance burdens.

Thus, when the FTC was developing its final record-keeping requirements for insulation sellers in aid of its rule requiring uniform disclosure of measured insulating value, it heeded the concerns of the small entrepreneurial cellulose insulation sellers, who felt that record-keeping requirements suitable for the industrial giants who marketed fiberglass insulation would be disproportionately burdensome for the small cellulose producers.[12]

When the Senate was considering Senator Philip Hart's original fair-packaging-and-labeling bill,[13] which would have mandated standard sizes for grocery products, I was the young staff member and consumer enthusiast assigned to the bill for the Senate Commerce Committee. Bryce Harlow, that marvelously subtle and persuasive advocate, then representing Procter & Gamble, came around to see me. Standardization of sizes, he said, would pose no particular difficulty for Procter & Gamble, but it would for various smaller competitors, such as the local cookie manufacturer, whose 15¼-ounce package competed with P&G's 16-ounce package, and for whom that ¾-ounce difference might well provide the margin of competitive survival.

In that case, the benefits of preserving small, inefficient competitors were not persuasive, weighed against the calculated deception of consumers, and we were not swayed by the argument, though I was touched by P&G's concern for small business. But the adverse differential impact of regulation upon smaller competitors, when added to the differential tax and other burdens imposed by government on small businesses, which do not relate to the relative efficiency of those businesses, must be a concern of the regulator—at least in shaping remedies and regulatory requirements in such a way as to minimize that differential. When firms or whole industries offer only token resistance to nominally stiff regulation, it may be that they hear a small voice suggesting that the regulation may dampen pesky competition. This is, incidently, one of the intrinsic benefits of a combined consumer protection and antitrust agency such as the FTC, in which internal voices are heard on behalf both of remedying consumer injury and of competition.

12. 16 C.F.R. § 460 (1981).
13. U.S., Congress, Senate, 89th Cong., 2d sess., 1965, S. 985. Enacted into law November 3, 1966 (Fair Packaging and Labeling Act, Pub. L. No. 89–755, 80 Stat. 1296).

6. *Does the regulation preserve freedom of informed individual choice to the maximum extent consistent with consumer welfare?*

The regulator must respect the manifest preference of Americans for free and informed choice over government intrusion that constrains choice.

In what regulator's bosom does there not dwell a latent "nanny," solicitous of the health and well-being of his or her fellow citizens, fearful of senseless risk, ready to reach for regulatory swaddling clothes at the first sign of a sniffle, chicken soup at the ready? This regulatory itch must be resisted.

The same Opinion Research Corporation poll that confirmed great and growing popular support for consumer regulation simultaneously recorded the distinct preference of Americans for informed consumer choice.[14]

Take the case of product safety. Where hazards are latent; where products are purchased infrequently, their characteristics unfamiliar to consumers or subject to rapid technological change; where the risks of product failure are severe; or where minimum safe performance standards will force significant scale economies in safe design—in those circumstances, mandatory government safety standards may well be justified.

But where these conditions do not exist, an appropriate regulatory humility should dictate a preference for remedies that rely upon informed consumer choice, rather than the elimination of choices deemed undesirable by government decision makers.

Far from being a weak incentive, information in the hands of motivated consumers can prove far more potent in channeling market forces than fixed standards. Note the impact of comparative mileage ratings for new automobiles, which focused consumer demand for fuel-efficient passenger cars and helped force the auto manufacturers far beyond the levels set in mandatory fuel-efficiency standards. There is at least anecdotal evidence that the new energy-efficiency labels for major home appliances have similarly channeled competition in such appliances toward greater energy-efficiency performance. The commission's testing and ranking

14. In a January 1981 poll taken by the Opinion Research Corporation, a total of 82 percent of respondents surveyed said that they agreed or strongly agreed that "the proper role of the federal government is to see that consumers are provided with enough information so that they can decide for themselves which products and services to buy." (*ORC Public Opinion Index: Report to Management*, vol. 39, nos. 1 and 2 [Princeton, N.J.: Opinion Research Corporation, January 1981], p. 13.)

of cigarette tar and nicotine yields, coupled with a requirement that the ratings be disclosed in all advertisements, have stimulated competition for progressively lower tar and nicotine levels—far lower, most certainly, than mandatory maximum tar and nicotine standards could have delivered.[15]

As a society, we claim to value citizen sovereignty and the responsible exercise of informed choice. This is a value that lies at the core of our faith in the possibility of a democratic society. It is a precondition for the success of our political system, as well as of our economic system. We are also concerned, properly, with the inequities that arise when information is asymmetric, when sellers gain a bargaining advantage because they possess greater knowledge than buyers. We see informational remedies as part of government's responsibility to redress this imbalance between producers and consumers.

While consumers may theoretically not be willing to pay for information they are not accustomed to using, the very provision of that information may serve to educate consumers in its beneficial use. Consequently, the *ultimate* value of information to consumers is much higher than the *initial* value. Supermarket officials responded to the demands of consumer groups that price-per-unit markings be placed on supermarket shelves, though few consumers, at first, made use of the calculations. I have not seen recent data, but it would greatly surprise me if a substantial proportion of consumers have not now learned to use and rely upon price-per-unit comparisons. And as consumers learn to process information well in one context, those skills can be transferred to expand the range of informed choice in other consumer and citizen decisions.

Thus, in any case in which the advantage of required information disclosure is arguable from a narrow, economic cost-benefit standpoint, the regulator may be justified in giving the benefit of the doubt to mandatory information disclosure because of the generic social value of free choice and the tendency for information to become more valuable as its use becomes habitual.

7. *"States' rights" may be a tarnished symbol, but the federal regulator needs to ask, "To what extent is this problem appropriate for federal intervention and amenable to a centrally administered national standard?"*

15. See U.S. Department of Health and Human Services, *The Health Consequences of Smoking: The Changing Cigarette. A Report of the Surgeon General* (Washington, D.C.: Government Printing Office, 1981), pp. 195–237.

Appropriate regulatory humility encompasses restraint in federal intervention in decentralized industries composed of small local enterprises and restraint in the expansion of the growth and reach of centralized federal bureaucracy. Where federal action *is* appropriate, such humility also counsels simple, flexible, regulatory mechanisms policed, wherever practical, through citizen self-help or with the aid of local law-enforcement authorities.

During the past few years, the FTC has deliberately stripped proposed trade-regulation rules of those elaborate regulatory schemes that, however well-grounded upon evidence of pervasive deceptive practices, would nonetheless have drawn the commission into policing commitments that could only have been met by a vastly increased national army of FTC investigators and enforcers.

It was in large measure such considerations that led the commission to abandon provisions in its proposed funeral rule such as those that would have barred the display of the cheapest caskets in bizarre colors—though that variant of the "bait and switch" scheme was a well-documented part of the manipulative selling techniques through which the distraught arranger of a funeral was directed to the more expensive caskets.

These concerns also influenced the commission's decision to scrap the elaborate regulatory precautions proposed in its vocational rule. It would have taken an army of FTC inspectors to investigate the failure of vocational school salesmen to make accurate representations, or, worse, to discover and prove deceptive oral statements, however reprehensible. But a quick check of standard form contracts will disclose compliance with the pro rata refund provision—a provision that has the added benefit of promoting self-enforcement by students.

Concern for the limits of appropriate federal reach also led the commission to prepare and advocate the consideration of model state laws, amenable to variations depending on local customs and needs, in subject areas where the breadth and depth of FTC investigation and regulatory analysis was beyond the resources of any one state.

CONCLUSION

The critic A. J. Liebling plucked the feathers from some of our most preening columnists by unmasking their ritualistic equivocation. He labeled this ritual "Adamonai, Kodemonai," evoking the Japanese symbols for "on the one hand this" and "on the other hand that." This chapter might well have been appropriately entitled "The 'Adamonai, Kodemonai' of Economic Regulation." It certainly reveals unresolved tensions between newly absorbed regulatory lessons and old truths; between the elegance of the economist's models and the inelegant passion of moral outrage and indignation; between an individualistic ideology, enshrining the solution of social problems through individual choice, disciplining firms in self-interested economic combat, and what George C. Lodge has called the coming "communitarian" ideology.[16]

The problem, of course, is that untidy values clutter up the economist's ordered universe. Americans tend to be uncomfortable with intellectual clutter; they are captivated by the apparent precision of regulatory decision making through market models. On the other hand, writes William Pfaff, most Europeans are morally offended by the "implacable insistence" of Americans that "the market determine value even in political, intellectual and artistic arenas."

"Europeans," Pfaff continues, "regard the objectivity of the market as a disguise for abdication of values and of intellectual independence." And he cites Baudelaire, who wrote in his notebooks that the "ruin of republics" follows "the degradation of the human heart" that results from the "pitiless wisdom which condemns everything except money."[17]

Between the analytical niceties of cost-benefit analysis and the moral outrage of Baudelaire lie the battlegrounds of regulation.

16. Lodge, *The New American Ideology* (New York: Alfred A. Knopf, 1977), pp. 163–97.
17. Pfaff, "Elites and Egalitarians," *New Yorker,* September 28, 1981, p. 121.

EPILOGUE

Since I delivered the lectures in which this book originated, good friends have benevolently called my attention to flaws, inconsistencies, and ambivalences.

That the lectures should have reflected contrasting moods is not surprising. I plunged into retrospection in the very first days after the Reagan election. The lectures took form, seriatum, mostly in the spring, summer, and fall of 1981. Like an archaeologist sifting a shallow dig, I can now trace my shifting moods as the Reagan presidency evolved from promise (and threat) to actuality.

The first lecture reflected the nostalgia of an unceremoniously unhorsed bureaucrat for earlier green pastures. The second lecture more directly vented my own anger and alarm at the state of political grace achieved by the business lobbies. By the summer of 1981, business dominance of government decision making loomed even more menacing and unshakeable in the hands of an administration and Congress in perfect harmony with business desires. In the third lecture, written in the early fall, combativeness was stirring; and by the fourth lecture written shortly thereafter, fresh outrage and faint hope had been rekindled—muted, however, by a heightened awareness of the inherent limits of the old entrepreneurial strategies.

Several commentators noted that the contrition evident in the final lecture seems at war with the uncontrite consumer zealotry of the first four lectures. Quite so. That lecture cured slowly through-

153

out the year. It was an offering, if not a sacrifice, to the apostles of
regulatory reform. It was to be the answer to the exasperated critic
who demanded, "My God, hasn't he learned *anything* in eighteen
years pushing regulation?!"

I have made some fine windage corrections to reconcile apparent
inconsistencies, where possible. But real internal flaws that cannot
be papered over do exist. They should be faced.

One unresolved self-conflict centers around the relentlessly adversary stance of consumer entrepreneurial strategies—the politics
of outrage. Nelson Polsby particularly challenges my unqualified
admiration for Ralph Nader, viewing Nader as an apostle of incivil-
ity, undermining constructive public discourse.

In twenty years of political brawling, I have from time to time
been disconcerted to recognize decent (though benighted) impulses
lurking in an adversary's breast. And a small voice occasionally
breaks through the rhetoric of combat to urge that true problem
solving means bridging controversy, achieving empathy with adversaries, seeking common ground, compromise and accommodation, not polarization.

Then I reflect on the wreckage of past efforts at non-confronta-
tional accommodation.

And I think: what would have happened to the FTC's authorization bill in conference committee if Ralph Nader had not, Sherman-
like, marched through Wendell Ford's Kentucky and Jack Danforth's Missouri?

Our operational model is the old mule tamer, who proceeds bru-
tally to club the recalcitrant mule, heedless of the anguished entreaties of the farmer. "With a mule," he remarks in classic laconic
style, "the first thing is, you gotta get his attention."

I recall a most civil Aspen Institute seminar on the corporation
and society, where I found myself arguing waspishly that advertising to very young children was simply "immoral." Among the participants was Sir Hu Weldon, the former president of the BBC, who
had no trouble agreeing that television advertising to young children has no place in a civilized society. "It is," he pronounced,
"unseemly." But he objected strenuously to my insistence that the
practice be viewed as an example of corporate immorality. He
viewed me, he confided to another participant, as too "monklike."

Perhaps, like Nader, I have been quick to invoke moral judgment, which chills civil discourse. Yet I also believe, with Kazantzakis, that "every man owes himself the obligation of anger." In a

polity characterized by inequity, I find the obligation of outrage and the uses of civility irreconcilable.

This introduces a final troublesome ambivalence: the problem of reconciling optimism and pessimism.

My friend the journalist David Burnham, with characteristic clarity, observed after having read the draft lectures: "I cannot quite tell if you believe that the cup is half full or half empty; whether you are celebrating the triumphs of democracy and the public interest over great odds or abandoning hope."

There is much to be pessimistic about in the experiences that informed these lectures. Lindblom *is* right: even in the most representative of administrations, there has been a failure of equity in government decision making affecting business and consumers. Politicians and bureaucrats chronically hesitate to challenge business demands, especially when such demands are backed by implicit or explicit threats that business's role in maintaining prosperity will be otherwise impaired.

When an administration mesmerized by the virtues of business is coupled with a Congress both mesmerized and mortgaged to business it would seem logical to abandon hope.

In the wake of Ronald Reagan's electoral triumph, Ellen Goodman captured the cold awakening of the liberal:

> Now we know that some of the movements were nourished on heady air but had weak roots. We know that some have never survived hard times in our country. We know that some simply have strong enemies. And we know that it all now hangs in abeyance.

Yet liberals hope; it is their tradition; it is in their character. They can even find hope in the Reagan wreckage of liberal programs— ample fuel for anger and outrage to fire new movements. (Though in Reagan we seem to have met a presidential persona with a seemingly infinite capacity to baffle appropriate outrage.)

How can we take hope in the fragmentary evidence of a resurgent populism?

Yes, there is now ample evidence of an awakening populist animus. The rash gamble of the Reagan administration on the undirected capacity of the private sector to restore prosperity has failed. As confidence in business plummets, the government's redistribution of wealth to business and the owners of business has lost what little legitimacy supply-side economics may momentarily have provided. And, as most of us become poorer, issues of marketplace equity—consumer issues—grow more central to people's daily concerns.

In such circumstances, there is historical precedent for a resurgence of popular demand that business be made to serve the public interest. But it is also true that the history of populism in America has been shadowed by meanness of spirit, racism, and diversion to futile panaceas—the embracing of symptomatic, rather than systematic, solutions. Populism has often been characterized by alienation and distrust of government and institutional leadership—distrust born of bitter experience, to be sure.

The achievement of populist goals surely requires the restoration of some measure of faith in the integrity and capacity of government as the critical instrument of economic and social justice. Beating up on the bureaucracy, while enormously satisfying to rich and poor alike, is hardly a productive path to a fair and orderly redistribution of political and economic power from economic privilege to democratic responsiveness. There must be new links forged between people and a responsive bureaucracy. This is not quite so utopian as it sounds. Remember, we did catch a glimpse of such a link in the emerging bond between the FTC and the organized elderly, a growing feeling that the FTC was indeed *their* agency, responsive to *their* needs. But the gap between bureaucracy and popular will remains vast.

Joan Claybrook, without peer as an indefatigable worker for the consumer interest, was once asked: "What sustains you, in the face of so many defeats?" "Well," she paused, then brightened: "We don't always lose!"

That's not precisely optimism. It's not a clarion rallying cry. But it is enough to keep us going.

INDEX

157

Designer:	Janet Wood
Compositor:	Innovative Media
Printer:	Vail-Ballou Press
Binder:	Vail-Ballou Press
Text:	10/12 Palatino
Display:	Palatino